D1423088

Mother & Baby Animal
CROSS STITCH

Based on the paintings of

In association with

www.dmccreative.co.uk

David and Charles

www.rucraft.co.uk

DMC would like to thank Maria Diaz and Jenny Barton for their help with charting the designs.

A DAVID & CHARLES BOOK
Copyright © David & Charles Limited 2009

David & Charles is an F+W Media Inc. company
4700 East Galbraith Road
Cincinnati, OH 45236

First published in the UK and US in 2009

Layout and photography copyright © David & Charles 2009
Text and charted designs copyright © DMC Creative World Ltd 2009
Paintings, sketches and quotes by Pollyanna Pickering © Otter House
(Licensing) Limited 2009.

All rights reserved. No part of this publication may be reproduced, stored
in a retrieval system, or transmitted, in any form or by any means,
electronic or mechanical, by photocopying, recording or otherwise, without
prior permission in writing from the publisher.

The designs in this book are copyright and must not be stitched for resale.

The publisher has made every effort to ensure that all the instructions in
the book are accurate and safe, and therefore cannot accept liability for
any resulting injury, damage or loss to persons or property, however it
may arise.

Names of manufacturers, fabric ranges and other products are provided
for the information of readers, with no intention to infringe copyright
or trademarks.

A catalogue record for this book is available from the British Library.

ISBN-13: 978-0-7153-2989-4 hardback
ISBN-10: 0-7153-2989-8 hardback
ISBN-13: 978-0-7153-2990-0 paperback
ISBN-10: 0-7153-2990-1 paperback

Printed in China by R R Donnelley
for David & Charles
Brunel House   Newton Abbot   Devon

Senior Commissioning Editor: Cheryl Brown
Editor: Bethany Dymond
Assistant Editor: Kate Nicholson
Project Editor and Chart Preparation: Lin Clements
Designers: Eleanor Stafford and Sabine Eulau
Photographers: Kim Sayer and Karl Adamson
Production Controller: Kelly Smith

Visit our website at www.davidandcharles.co.uk

David & Charles books are available from all good bookshops; alternatively
you can contact our Orderline on 0870 9908222 or write to us at
FREEPOST EX2 110, D&C Direct, Newton Abbot, TQ12 4ZZ (no stamp
required UK only); US customers call 800-289-0963 and Canadian
customers call 800-840-5220.

Contents

Introducing Pollyanna Pickering

The vision and talent of internationally acclaimed artist Pollyanna Pickering is brought to the world of cross stitch with a truly wonderful collection of designs celebrating the remarkable and endearing relationship between animal mothers and their young.

"Many things can inspire the creation of a painting – the most important thing for me is the time spent sketching on location – these sketches then form the basis for my finished painting."

Pollyanna Pickering, the Artist

Pollyanna Pickering is widely recognized as Europe's foremost wildlife artist and is the most published fine artist working in Britain today. Pollyanna, who studied at London Central School of Art, is a patron of the Wildlife Art Society International. She has won many awards for both her art and her achievements in business and conservation and in 2008 received an honorary degree from Derby University. Her animal portraits are simply stunning and include lions, tigers, leopards, elephants, giraffes, wolves, meerkats and many varieties of birds.

Pollyanna's work has been exhibited in top galleries internationally, including the Royal Academy, and she has designed exclusively for Royal Doulton, Wedgwood and Harrods. Her limited-edition and fine-art prints, books, ranges of Christmas and greetings cards and giftware are sold throughout the UK and over 80 countries worldwide, which means that her work is familiar to most people. Since 1994 Pollyanna's work has been published by Otter House Limited. Pollyanna's daughter, Anna-Louise Pickering, works closely with her mother and has authored several books of their expeditions (see page 105 for details).

Inspired by her love of animals and the beauty of the natural world, Pollyanna has travelled to the most remote and inhospitable parts of the world to study and paint endangered species in their natural habitats. Her intrepid exhibitions have taken her across five continents, including the jungles of India and the wastelands of Siberia in search of tigers, the Tibetan borderlands of China to seek out giant pandas, to Namibia in Africa to study wild cheetahs and to the Canadian High Arctic to sketch polar bears. Pollyanna's passion to protect wildlife lead to the establishment of the Pollyanna Pickering Foundation in 2001, which raises funds for worldwide conservation, animal welfare and disaster relief.

"When I travel I am able to experience the natural world in all its beauty, danger and drama. It is only through this first-hand study of animals and their habitats that I am able to paint in a way that communicates my love and respect for our remarkable, awe-inspiring but ultimately fragile world."

Pollyanna Pickering and DMC

DMC was established over 250 years ago and today is the leading thread manufacturing company. DMC manufacture the world's most widely used stranded cotton thread, as well as cross stitch and tapestry kits, fabrics, ready-to-stitch items and stitching accessories (see page 103). DMC's creative association with Pollyanna Pickering has brought her unique art to cross stitchers worldwide.

Translating Pollyanna's fabulous and realistic paintings into fabric and thread has resulted in a beautiful selection of cross stitch designs celebrating the special bond between animal mothers and their babies. These adorable portraits are sure to endear themselves to all cross stitch fans. So journey with Pollyanna to the most far-flung corners of the globe as you stitch these irresistible designs.

"I love seeing the adaptation of my work into cross stitch designs. It fascinates me how my brushstrokes can be converted so effectively into stitch work to recreate the forms, shapes and tones of my paintings."

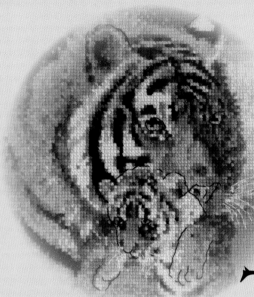

Tiger

Native to eastern and southern Asia, the tiger is the largest and most powerful of the big cats and certainly one of the most impressive creatures on the planet. They prefer a forest habitat but can also be found in grasslands and swamps. Unlike other big cats they are fond of water and are good swimmers. Tigers are easily recognized by their cream throat and belly and fabulous orange coat covered with thick black stripes. No two tigers have the same striped pattern on their coats.

Female tigers bear litters of three or four cubs, each about 1kg (2lb) and rear them alone, avoiding wandering male tigers that may kill the cubs in order to make the female receptive to mating. The cubs are guarded fiercely by their mother until they are 18 months old when they become independent, but they continue to stay under her protection until they are about two years old. After this time she will have taught them all the skills they need to survive and seek territory of their own.

What safer place could there be than under the protection of a magnificent mother tiger? A cub soon learns to do as he is told and just hang on in there. A second design on page 11 shows the little one venturing out for the first time.

Special Delivery

A mother tiger is very protective of her cubs, although moving them to a safer location might not be the most dignified way to travel! The snowy wastes depicted in this fabulous design remind us how wide ranging the tiger's territory is.

STITCH COUNT
160h x 128w

DESIGN SIZE
25.4 x 20.3cm (10 x 8in)

YOU WILL NEED
🌿 46 x 40.5cm (18 x 16in)
16-count Aida in light blue
(DMC code 800)
🌿 DMC stranded cotton (floss)
as listed in chart key (1 skein of
each colour and 2 skeins of 803
and 931)
🌿 DMC Light Effects E168
and Satin thread S800 (1 skein
of each)
🌿 Tapestry needle size 24–26
🌿 Suitable picture frame

1 Prepare your fabric and threads for work and mark the centre point on the fabric and on the chart on pages 14/15.

2 Follow the chart and work over one block of Aida, using two strands for whole and three-quarter cross stitches. Work French knots and backstitches with one strand.

3 When all stitching is complete, check for missed stitches and then remove any guidelines used. Mount and frame your picture as desired.

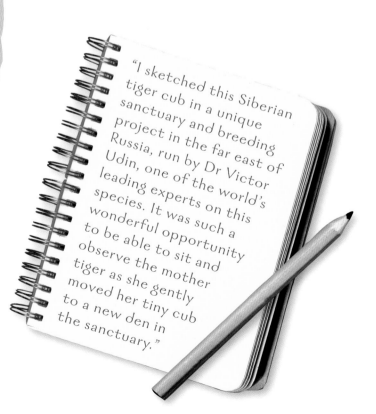

"I sketched this Siberian tiger cub in a unique sanctuary and breeding project in the far east of Russia, run by Dr Victor Udin, one of the world's leading experts on this species. It was such a wonderful opportunity to be able to sit and observe the mother tiger as she gently moved her tiny cub to a new den in the sanctuary."

First Snow

Could there be a cuter picture? This sweet design of a cub venturing out into the snow for the first time will always attract attention. DMC Satin thread in white has been used in places to bring a shine to snowy areas.

STITCH COUNT
80h x 112w

DESIGN SIZE
12.7 x 17.8cm (5 x 7in)

YOU WILL NEED
- 33 x 38cm (13 x 15in) 16-count Aida in light blue (DMC code 800)
- DMC stranded cotton (floss) and Satin thread as listed in chart key (1 skein of each colour)
- Tapestry needle size 24–26
- Suitable picture frame

1 Prepare your fabric and threads for work and mark the centre point on the fabric and on the chart on page 13.

2 Follow the chart and work over one block of Aida, using two strands for whole and three-quarter cross stitches. Work backstitches with one strand.

3 When all stitching is complete, check for missed stitches and then remove any guidelines used. Mount and frame your picture as desired.

"In my quest to paint the Siberian tiger I travelled to the far east of Russia, where the temperatures dropped to a bone-chilling minus 40° centigrade. I stayed with a beekeeper and his wife in a tiny wooden cabin deep in the forest, where there was no electricity, no running water and no inside loo!"

DMC stranded
cotton
Cross stitch
(2 strands)

	762	898	930	931	932	3051	3752	3862	3864	blanc	Satin S5200
310	317	318	413	415	433	434	435	436	437	738	739	

Backstitch
(1 strand)
— 310
— 415
— 840
— blanc

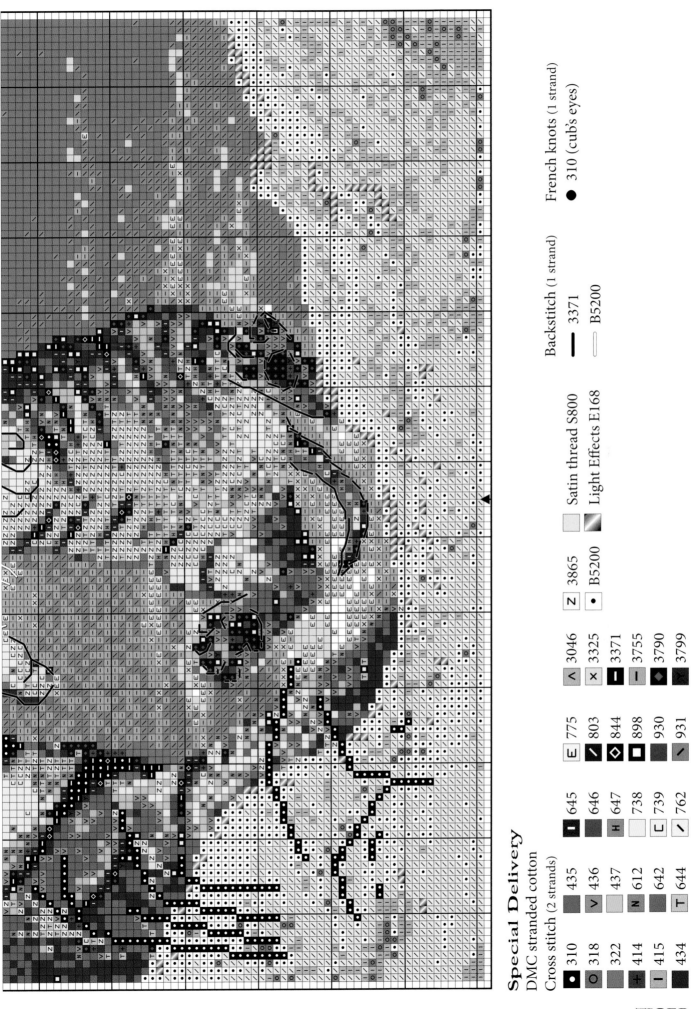

Special Delivery

DMC stranded cotton

Cross stitch (2 strands)

⊡ 310	**■** 645	**E** 775	**<** 3046
○ 318	**V** 646	**◱** 803	**×** 3325
322	**H** 647	**◈** 844	**▮** 3371
+ 414	738	**□** 898	**I** 3755
I 415	**⊔** 739	**◆** 930	**◆** 3790
■ 434	**/** 762	**◢** 931	**◣** 3799
■ 435			
V 436			
437			
N 612			
⊔ 642			
T 644			

Z 3865   Satin thread S800

• B5200   Light Effects E168

Backstitch (1 strand)

— 3371

— B5200

French knots (1 strand)

● 310 (cub's eyes)

White Tiger

Sightings of wild white tigers were first made in the early 19th century and these rare, magnificent creatures have captured public attention ever since. A white tiger is not a separate subspecies of tiger or an albino but a white-coloured Bengal tiger, the result of two parents with a genetic mutation. White tigers often have blue eyes and pink noses and the most distinctive coat of creamy-white fur with pale chocolate-coloured stripes. Their unusual colouration has made them popular with zoos and currently there are several hundred in captivity worldwide.

Like other female tigers, white tigers make formidable mothers and bear litters of two or three cubs, which tend to be heavier at birth than normal Bengal tigers. The mother guards her cubs fiercely, keeping them in the protection of a den until they are about two months old. After that they leave the den and follow their mother, learning the stalking and hunting skills they will need when they venture out on their own at about two years old.

The rare and unusual colouring of white tigers makes them a fabulous subject for a cross stitch design. Their exotic coats and regal bearing are captured beautifully in this picture.

Mother Love

Working this touching scene on black fabric allows the white fur of the tigers to glow amid the darkness all around them. Stitching the background in half cross stitch adds depth to the design.

STITCH COUNT
130h x 166w

DESIGN SIZE
23.5 x 30cm (9¼ x 12in)

YOU WILL NEED
- 43 x 51cm (17 x 20in) 14-count Aida in black (DMC code 310)
- DMC stranded cotton (floss) as listed in chart key (1 skein of each colour and 2 skeins of 415)
- Suitable picture frame

1 Prepare your fabric and threads for work and mark the centre point on the fabric and on the chart on pages 20–23.

2 Follow the chart and work over one block of Aida, using three strands for B5200 full and three-quarter cross stitches and two strands for all other cross stitches. Use two strands for half cross stitch and work backstitches with one strand.

3 When all stitching is complete, check for missed stitches and then remove any guidelines used. Mount and frame your picture as desired.

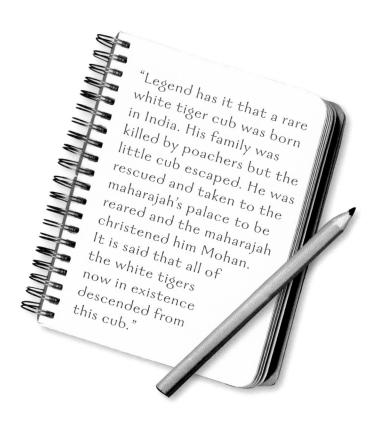

"Legend has it that a rare white tiger cub was born in India. His family was killed by poachers but the little cub escaped. He was rescued and taken to the maharajah's palace to be reared and the maharajah christened him Mohan. It is said that all of the white tigers now in existence descended from this cub."

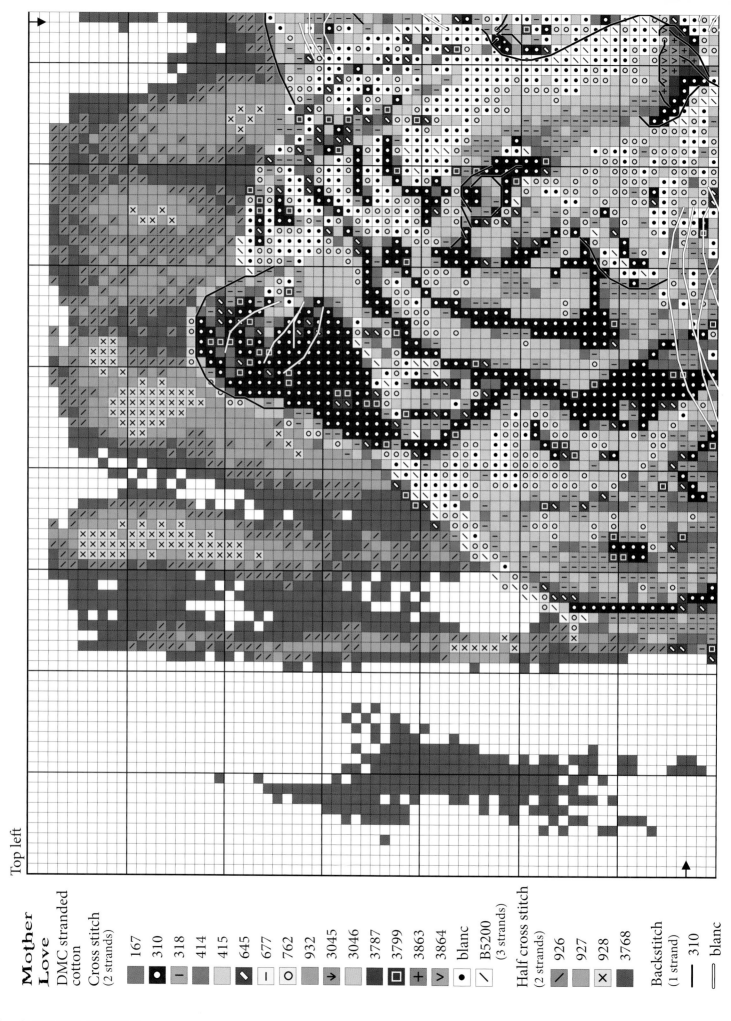

Mother Love

DMC stranded cotton

Cross stitch (2 strands)

	167
	310
	318
	414
	415
	645
	677
	762
	932
	3045
	3046
	3787
	3799
	3863
	3864
	blanc
	B5200 (3 strands)

Half cross stitch (2 strands)

	926
	927
	928
	3768

Backstitch (1 strand)

——	310
——	blanc

Top left

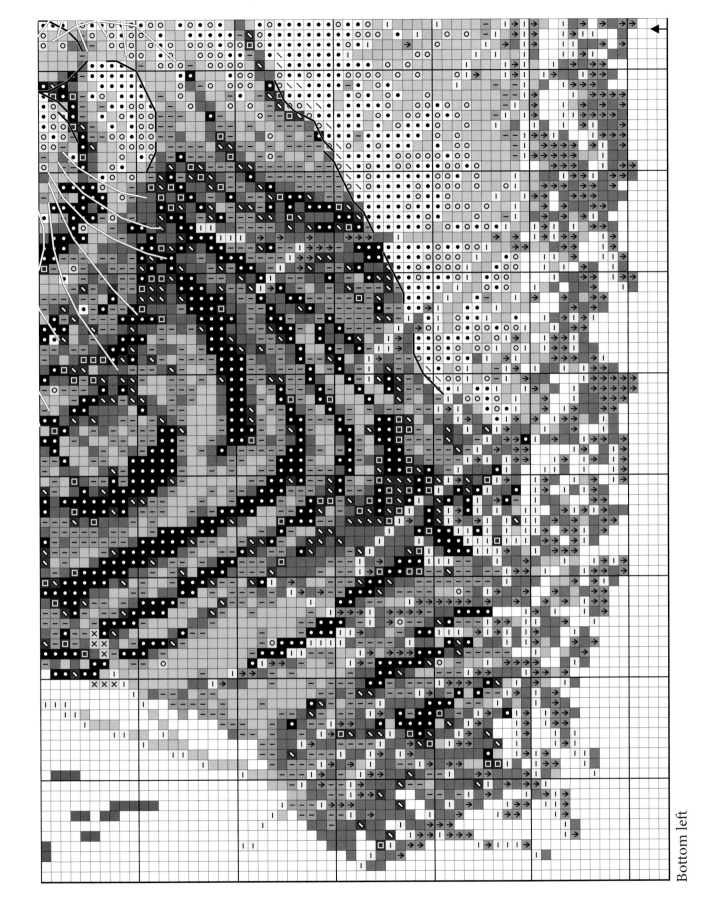

Mother Love

DMC stranded cotton

Cross stitch
(2 strands)

■	167
■●	310
—	318
■	414
■	415
◣	645
I	677
○	762
→	932
■	3045
■	3046
■	3787
⊡	3799
+	3863
∨	3864
●	blanc
◺	B5200

Half cross stitch
(3 strands)
(2 strands)

╱	926
▨	927
✕	928
■	3768

Backstitch
(1 strand)

——	310
——	blanc

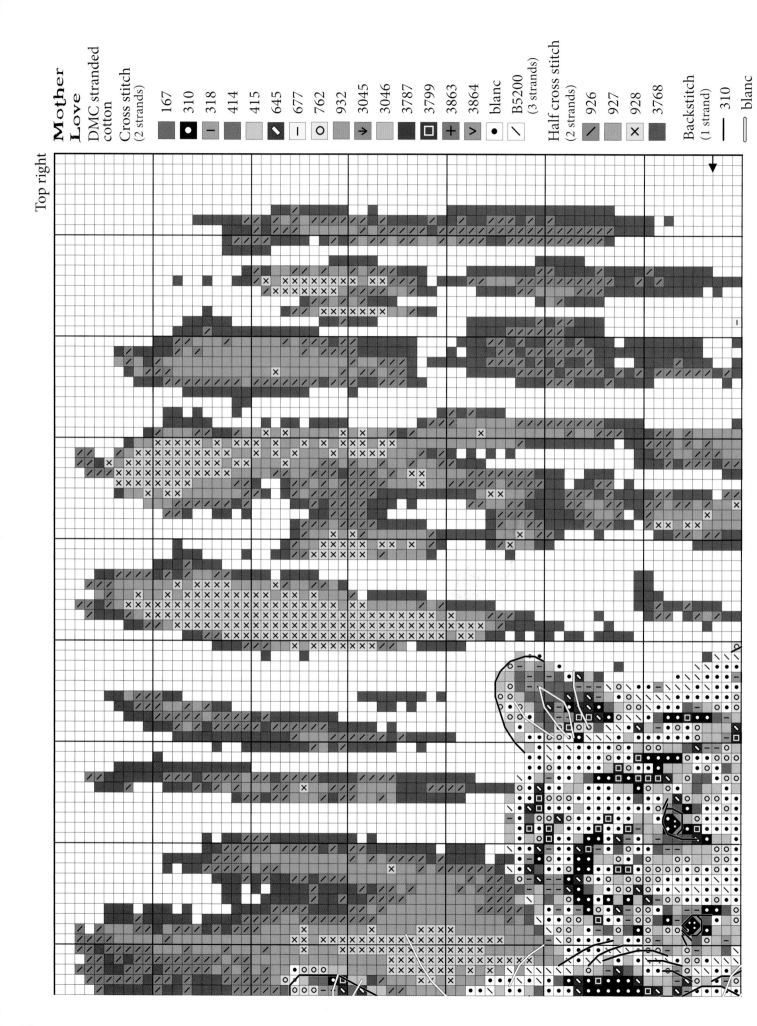

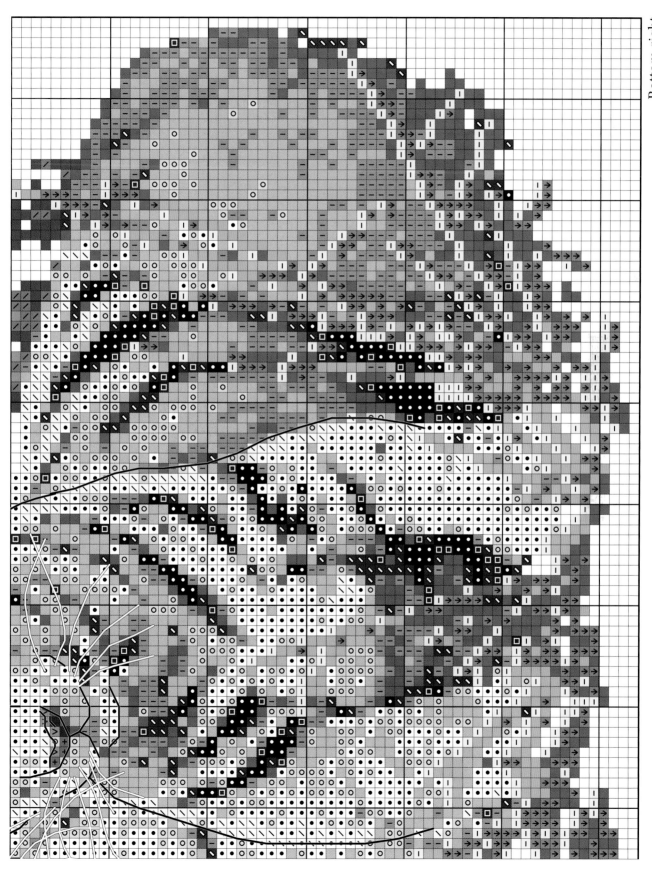

Panda

The panda is instantly recognizable the world over by the distinctive black patches around its eyes, ears and across its round body. Its look of innocence and docile nature have made it a great favourite. Native to China, where it is considered a rare and noble creature, the panda's diet is 99% bamboo and a panda will eat 9–14kg (20–30lbs) of various types of bamboo shoots a day.

Female pandas bear only one young every two years, which partly explains their endangered status worldwide. At birth, baby pandas are extremely small and helpless, weighing only 90–130g (3¼–4½oz) and so are utterly dependent on their mother. Female pandas make devoted mothers, cradling their cub in giant paws and comforting them with little pats and nuzzles. As the cub grows older they play with their mother by rolling and wrestling. Although relying on their mother's milk for the first year, a cub will begin to eat bamboo after six months but stays in a close relationship with its mother until nearly two years old.

The panda's peaceful nature and love of play are portrayed in this delightful scene. The design is stitched on dark blue Aida, which adds to the intimate atmosphere. Another adorable design, a little cub just waking from sleep, is featured on page 29.

Bear Hug

This endearing design is great fun to stitch. The changing colours of the DMC Color Variations threads create a realistic dappled look to the vegetation, while the use of a beautiful dark blue Aida provides an attractive contrast.

STITCH COUNT
112h x 140w

DESIGN SIZE
20.3 x 25.5cm (8 x 10in)

YOU WILL NEED
- 40.5 x 46cm (16 x 18in) 14-count Aida in dark blue (DMC code 796)
- DMC stranded cotton (floss) and Color Variations thread as listed in chart key (1 skein of each colour)
- Tapestry needle size 24–26
- Suitable picture frame

1 Prepare your fabric and threads for work and mark the centre point on the fabric and on the chart on pages 30/31.

2 Follow the chart and work over one block of Aida, using two strands for whole cross stitches and two strands for half cross stitches. Work backstitches with one strand.

3 When all stitching is complete, check for missed stitches and then remove any guidelines used. Mount and frame your picture as desired.

"My first book, Giant Pandas and Sleeping Dragons (see page 105), tells the story of my travels into China to paint the endangered giant pandas. While in this area I was fortunate enough to see a wild panda high in the mountains."

Sleepyhead

A panda cub waking from sleep makes the most adorable cross stitch design. The use of Color Variation thread creates a realistic mottled green background. The design would also make a lovely little cushion for a child's room.

STITCH COUNT
132h x 109w

DESIGN SIZE
24 x 19.8cm (9½ x 7¾in)

YOU WILL NEED
- 43 x 40.5cm (17 x 16in) 14-count Aida in pale green (DMC code 738)
- DMC stranded cotton (floss) as listed in chart key (1 skein of each colour)
- DMC Satin thread and Color Variations as listed in chart key (1 skein of each colour)
- Tapestry needle size 24—26
- Suitable picture frame

1 Prepare your fabric and threads for work and mark the centre point on the fabric and on the chart on pages 32/33.

2 Follow the chart and work over one block of Aida, using two strands for whole and three-quarter cross stitches. Work backstitches with one strand.

3 When all stitching is complete, check for missed stitches and then remove any guidelines used. Mount and frame your picture as desired.

"I worked in a panda hospital on the borderlands of Tibet where this orphaned baby panda was being cared for. Each day we would give him his bottle of yak's milk with honey and vitamins. This painting was done when he was six months old – he was feeling sleepy and rubbing his eyes just before his afternoon nap."

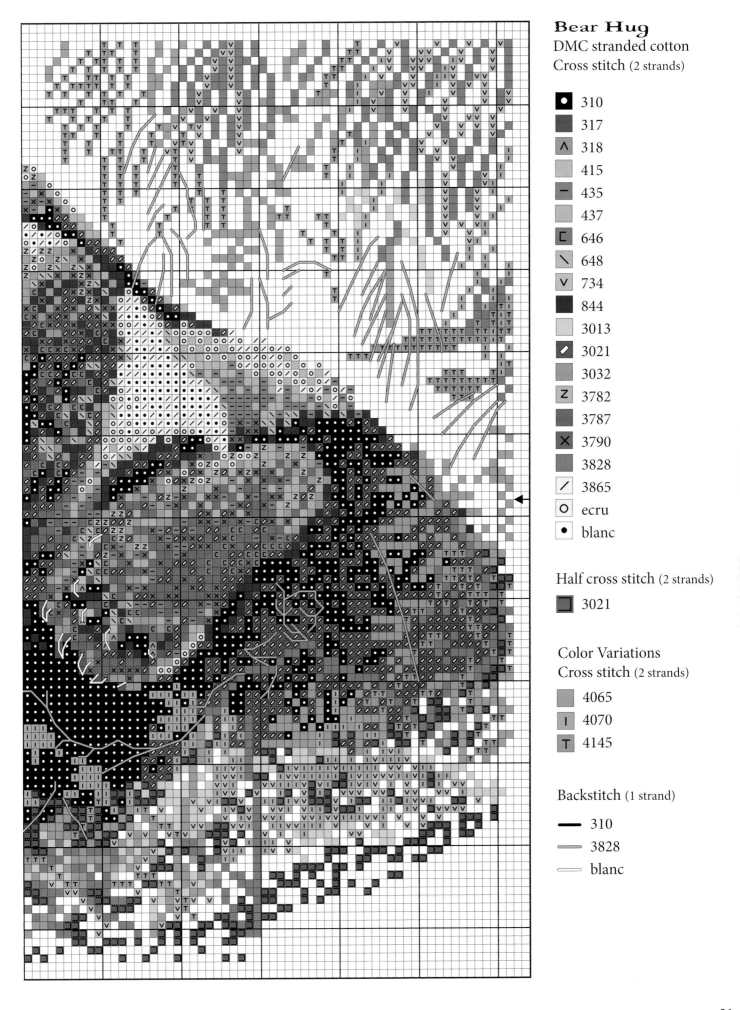

Bear Hug

DMC stranded cotton
Cross stitch (2 strands)

- 310
- 317
- 318
- 415
- 435
- 437
- 646
- 648
- 734
- 844
- 3013
- 3021
- 3032
- 3782
- 3787
- 3790
- 3828
- 3865
- ecru
- blanc

Half cross stitch (2 strands)

- 3021

Color Variations
Cross stitch (2 strands)

- 4065
- 4070
- 4145

Backstitch (1 strand)

- 310
- 3828
- blanc

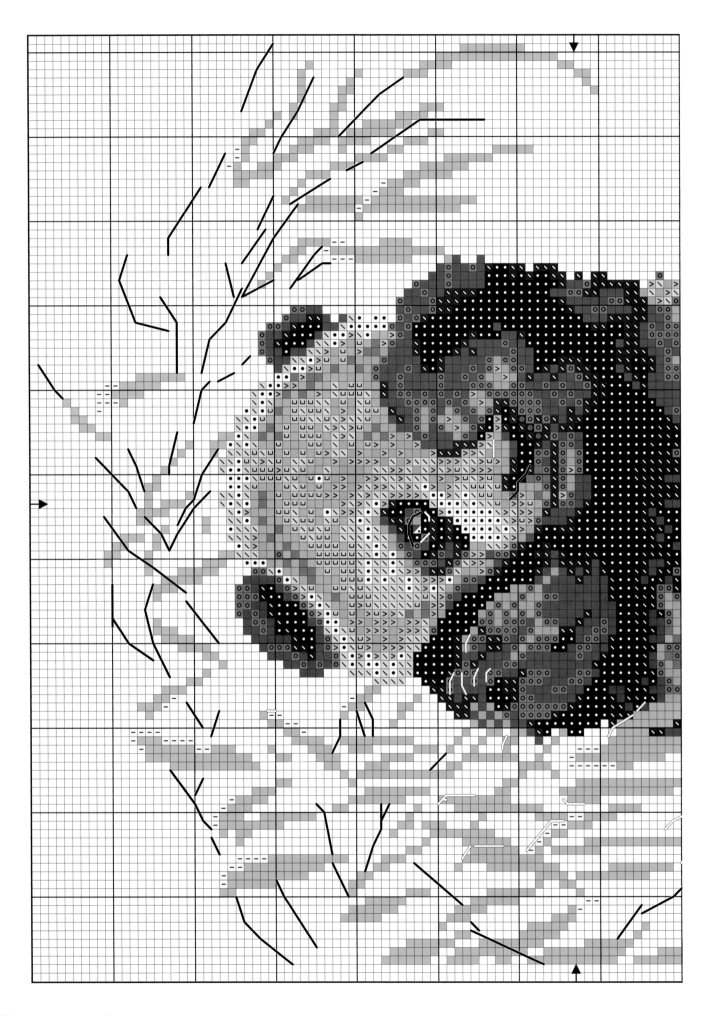

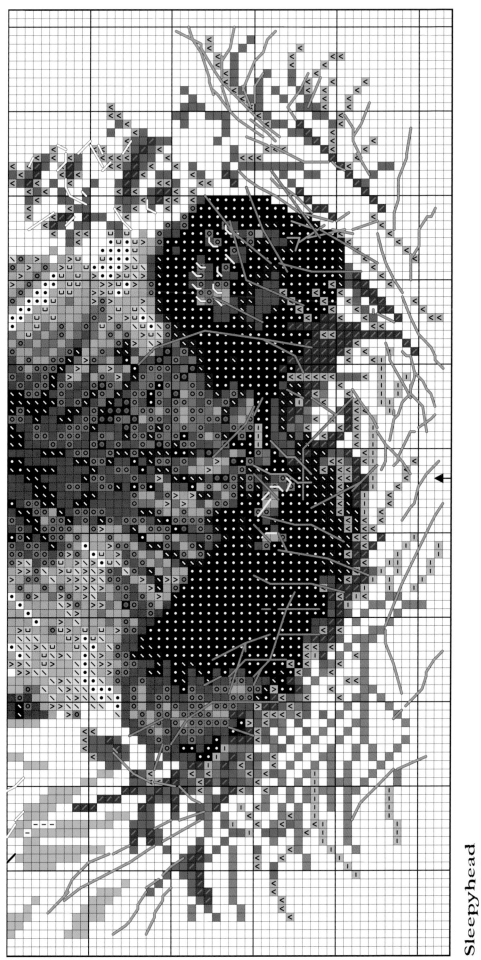

Sleepyhead

DMC stranded cotton

Cross stitch (2 strands)

◨	310	∨	415	
	318		436	
	413	−	437	
◉	414	⁄	762	

◪	3021		3362	
◉	3022		3363	
	3023	⟨	3364	
⊏	3024	◪	3799	

●	blanc			
	Satin S5200			
∣	Color Variations 4070			

Backstitch (1 strand)

——	310
——	436
——	471
——	blanc

Polar Bear

The magnificent polar bear is the world's largest land predator – twice as big as a Siberian tiger – and can be found over a vast area of the Arctic Ocean. Polar bears spend most of their time on the frozen sea, using their extraordinary sense of smell and swimming abilities to hunt seals.

Mating takes place on the sea ice in April and May, although the fertilized egg remains suspended within the female until August or September. This gives the mother-to-be time to put on the weight she needs to sustain her – she may not be able to hunt again for up to eight months. Cubs, usually twins, are born in a maternal den dug deeply into snowdrifts and are fed on fat-rich milk. Polar bear mothers are affectionate towards their young and will defend them fiercely. The cubs are very playful and as they grow older they play-fight, to develop the skills they will need when they have to survive alone, usually after about two and a half years.

This touching scene illustrates the affectionate bond that exists between a polar bear mother and her cub. Deep in the den cubs are fed and protected for more than two months. A second design on page 39 shows a plump young bear venturing out on his own.

Circle of Life

This delightful picture is a pleasure to stitch. The design is given a lovely gleam, like sunshine on snow, by the use of shiny Satin thread. The pale blue linen and background stitched in half cross stitch give depth to the design.

STITCH COUNT
112h x 140w

DESIGN SIZE
20.3 x 25.4cm (8 x 10in)

YOU WILL NEED
- 40.5 x 46cm (16 x 18in) 28-count linen in pale blue (DMC code 3840)
- DMC stranded cotton (floss) as listed in chart key (1 skein of each colour and 2 skeins of 3838)
- DMC Satin thread (1 skein)
- Suitable picture frame

1 Prepare your fabric and threads for work and mark the centre point on the fabric and on the chart on pages 40/41.

2 Follow the chart and work over one two linen threads, using two strands for whole cross stitches and two strands for half cross stitches. Use three strands for the Satin thread half cross stitches.

3 When all stitching is complete, check for missed stitches and then remove any guidelines used. Mount and frame your picture as desired.

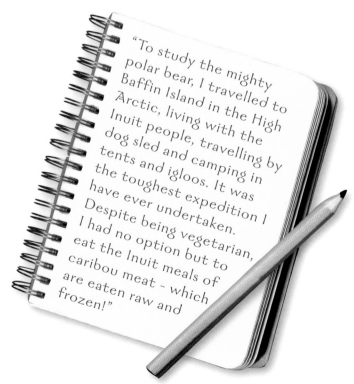

"To study the mighty polar bear, I travelled to Baffin Island in the High Arctic, living with the Inuit people, travelling by dog sled and camping in tents and igloos. It was the toughest expedition I have ever undertaken. Despite being vegetarian, I had no option but to eat the Inuit meals of caribou meat - which are eaten raw and frozen!"

Water Baby

A young bear beginning to fend for himself soon gets used to icy-cold water and the snowy wastes of the Arctic. Light Effects thread and Satin thread create the extra sparkle of glistening ice in this design.

STITCH COUNT
125h x 98w

DESIGN SIZE
23 x 18cm (9 x 7in)

YOU WILL NEED
- 43 x 38cm (17 x 15in) 14-count Aida in iridescent blue (DMC code 800)
- DMC stranded cotton (floss) as listed in chart key (1 skein of each colour)
- DMC Light Effects thread and Satin thread as listed in chart key (1 skein of each colour)
- Tapestry needle size 24–26
- Suitable picture frame

1 Prepare your fabric and threads for work and mark the centre point on the fabric and on the chart on pages 42/43.

2 Follow the chart and work over one block of Aida, using two strands for whole and three-quarter cross stitches and two strands for half cross stitches. Work backstitches with one strand.

3 When all stitching is complete, check for missed stitches and then remove any guidelines used. Mount and frame your picture as desired.

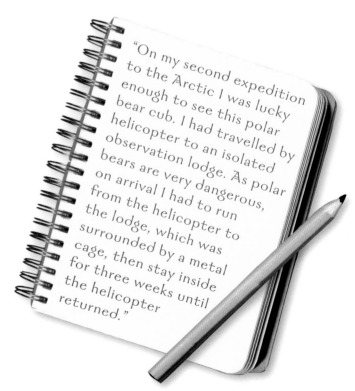

"On my second expedition to the Arctic I was lucky enough to see this polar bear cub. I had travelled by helicopter to an isolated observation lodge. As polar bears are very dangerous, on arrival I had to run from the helicopter to the lodge, which was surrounded by a metal cage, then stay inside for three weeks until the helicopter returned."

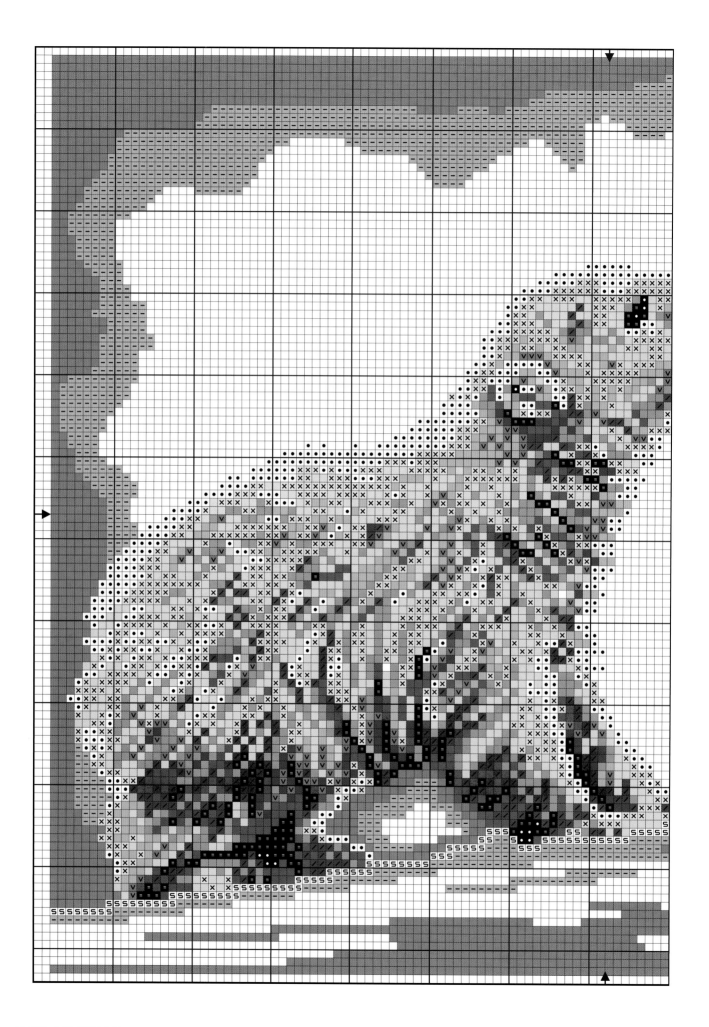

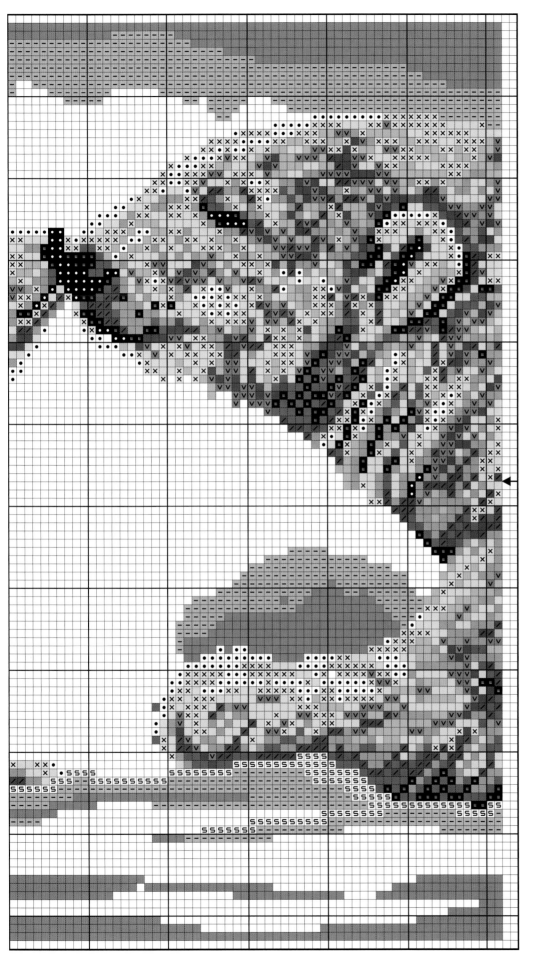

DMC stranded cotton

Cross stitch (2 strands)

◉	310
▨	317
▧	318
▣	413
◪	414
▢	415
▨	640
V	642
▨	644
✕	762
•	blanc

Half cross stitch

▨	3838 (2 strands)
—	3839 (2 strands)
S	Satin S5200 (3 strands)

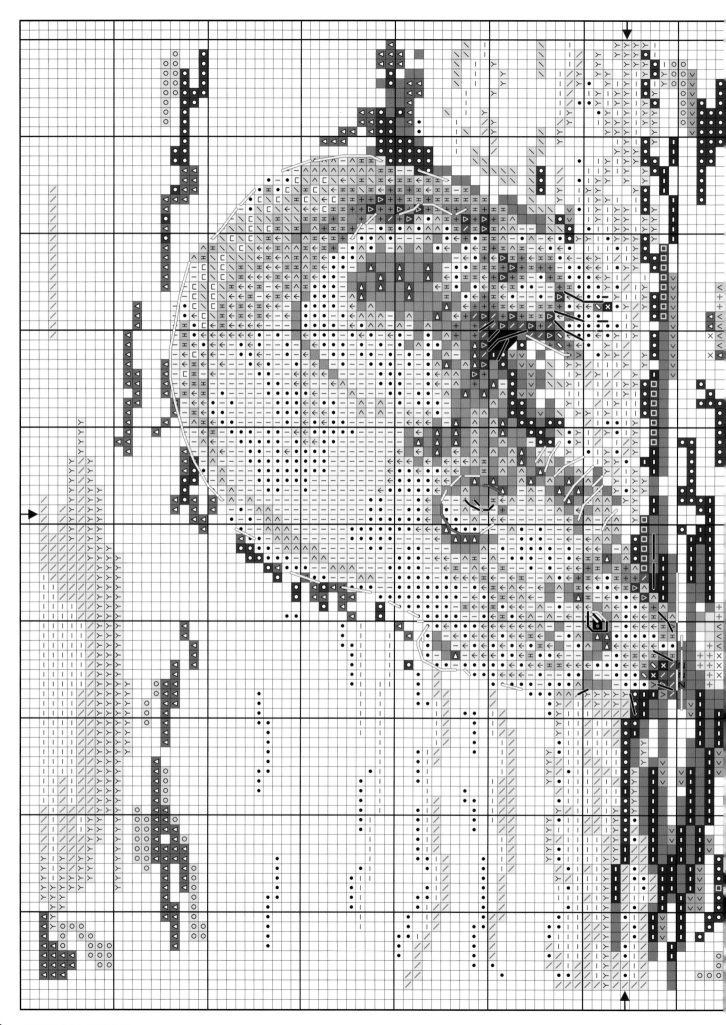

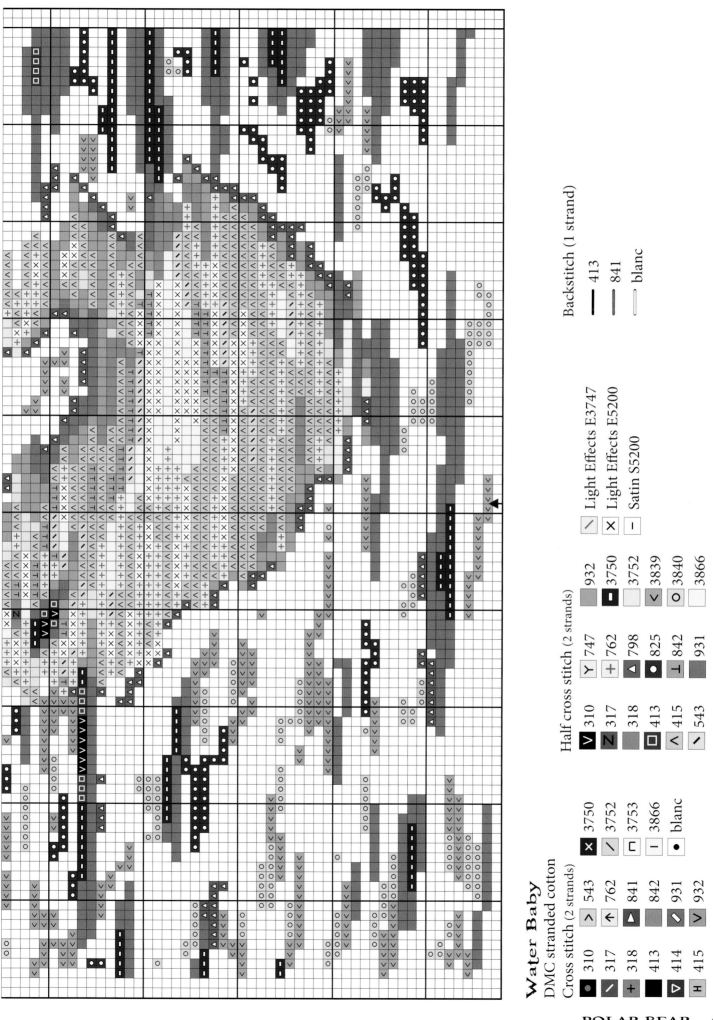

Water Baby
DMC stranded cotton

Cross stitch (2 strands)

◖ 310	✕ 3750	
╱ 317	╱ 3752	
✚ 318	⊓ 3753	
■ 413	— 3866	
▷ 414	● blanc	
H 415		

Half cross stitch (2 strands)

› 543	✕ 3750	
← 762	╱ 3752	
◮ 841	⊓ 3753	
◩ 842	— 3866	
◇ 931	● blanc	
∨ 932		

∨ 310	⍱ 932	
N 317	◧ 3750	
318	3752	
⊡ 413	◣ 3839	
‹ 415	○ 3840	
╱ 543	3866	
Y 747		
✚ 762		
◀ 798		
● 825		
⊤ 842		
931		

Light Effects E3747 ╱
Light Effects E5200 ✕
Satin S5200 —

Backstitch (1 strand)

— 413
— 841
⌒ blanc

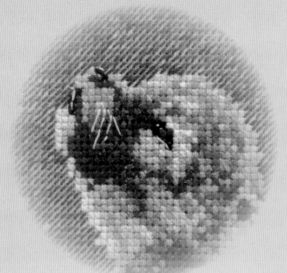

Wolf

The grey wolf is one of nature's survivors and is highly adaptable, able to thrive in tundra, forests, deserts, grasslands and even urban areas, although its range now is much limited due to human activity. Wolves are supreme predators and hunt very efficiently in packs of up to 30 members.

Wolves usually breed once a year from December to April and a pregnancy lasts around 63 days. The average litter size is four to six cubs, although the mother may have as many as ten. A cub weighs only about 0.5kg (1lb) at birth and cannot see or hear, so is totally dependent on its mother for food and protection. The mother will have prepared a den for her cubs and they live here alone for about two months, surviving on her milk and then regurgitated food. When they eventually leave the den to join the pack the lively pups are protected for some weeks by the mother and other adults and actively join in the hunt at about eight months old.

An ice-age survivor, the wolf can still be found in the Alaskan wilderness and this atmospheric design conjures up that cold, lonely environment. The safety and security that a mother wolf provides is portrayed in a second design on pages 48/49.

Singing Lesson

This design conveys the lifestyle of the wolf perfectly – mother and cub howling to other wolves, their pale breath visible against the bitterly cold night. Extensive areas of half cross stitch conjure up the dark velvet night.

STITCH COUNT
192h x 128w

DESIGN SIZE
30.5 x 20.3cm (12 x 8in)

YOU WILL NEED
- 51 x 40.5cm (20 x 16in) 16-count Aida in ecru (DMC code Ecru)
- DMC stranded cotton (floss) as listed in chart key (1 skein of each of colour, 2 skeins of 645 and 3 skeins of 535)
- Tapestry needle size 24–26
- Suitable picture frame

1 Prepare your fabric and threads for work and mark the centre point on the fabric and on the chart on pages 50–53.

2 Follow the chart and work over one block of Aida, using two strands for whole cross stitches and two strands for half cross stitches. Work backstitches with one strand.

3 When all stitching is complete, check for missed stitches and then remove any guidelines used. Mount and frame your picture as desired.

"Wolves are a favourite subject of mine. I travelled into the Carpathian Mountains of Transylvania, home to the highest density of European wolves, to paint these magnificent creatures. I have also sketched them in Canada and North America. I'm planning to paint the highly endangered Ethiopian wolf."

Earth Mother

A devoted wolf mother and her cubs snuggle together for warmth and companionship in the security of the mother's den. Using Color Variations thread creates subtle changes of colour in the foreground and background.

STITCH COUNT
99h x 196w

DESIGN SIZE
18 x 35.5cm (7 x 14in)

YOU WILL NEED

- 38 x 56cm (15 x 22in) 14-count Aida in black (DMC code 310)
- DMC stranded cotton (floss) and Color Variations thread as listed in chart key (1 skein of each colour and 2 skeins of 317, 318, 413, 414 and 415)
- Tapestry needle size 24–26
- Suitable picture frame

1 Prepare your fabric and threads for work and mark the centre point on the fabric and on the chart on pages 54/55.

2 Follow the chart and work over one block of Aida, using two strands for whole and three-quarter cross stitches and two strands for half cross stitches. Work backstitches with one strand.

3 When all stitching is complete, check for missed stitches and then remove any guidelines used. Mount and frame your picture as desired.

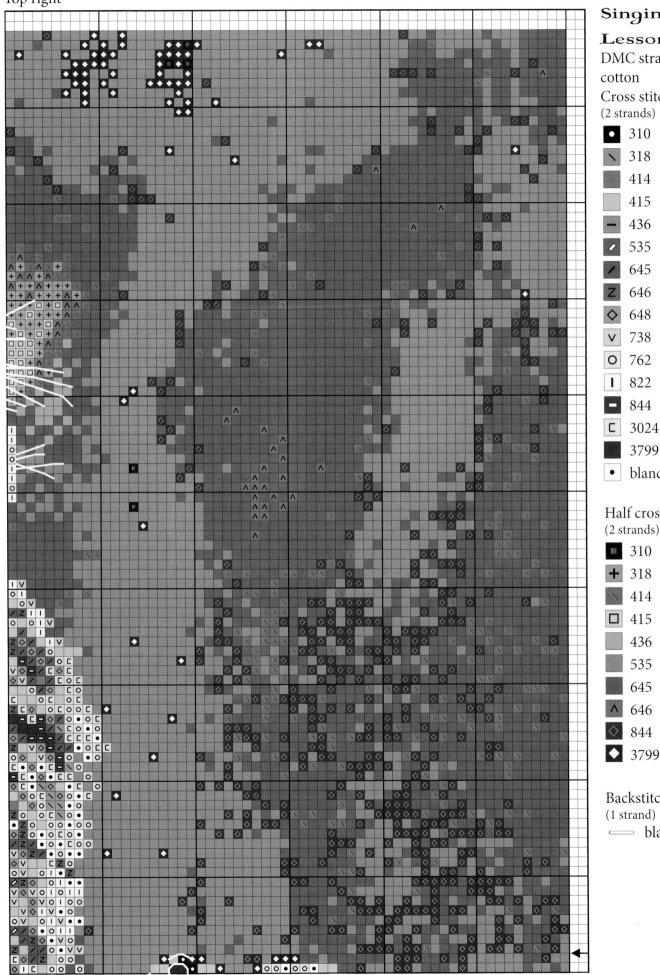

Singing Lesson

DMC stranded cotton

Cross stitch
(2 strands)

⬤	310
\	318
	414
	415
−	436
/	535
/	645
Z	646
◇	648
V	738
O	762
I	822
−	844
C	3024
	3799
•	blanc

Half cross stitch
(2 strands)

▣	310
+	318
\	414
☐	415
	436
	535
	645
∧	646
◇	844
◆	3799

Backstitch
(1 strand)

— blanc

Bottom left

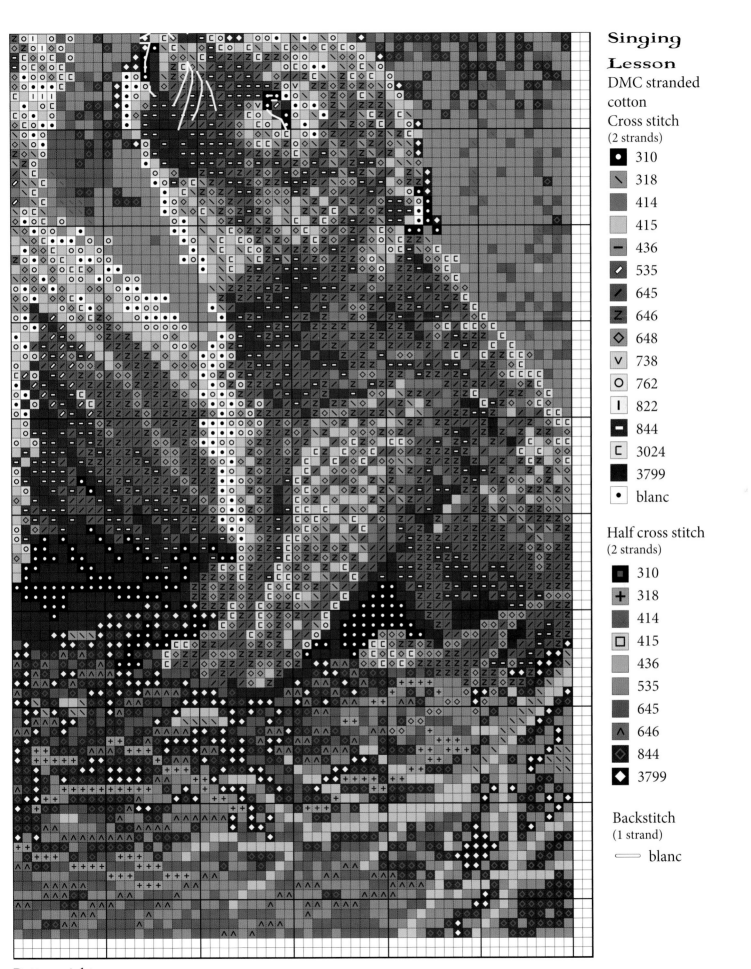

DMC stranded
cotton

Cross stitch
(2 strands)

⊡	310
╲	318
▨	414
▨	415
▬	436
◩	535
╱	645
Z	646
◇	648
V	738
O	762
I	822
▬	844
C	3024
▪	3799
•	blanc

Half cross stitch
(2 strands)

◼	310
+	318
▨	414
▢	415
▨	436
▨	535
▨	645
∧	646
◆	844
◆	3799

Backstitch
(1 strand)

⎯ blanc

Bottom right

Earth Mother

DMC stranded cotton

Cross stitch (2 strands)

- 310
- 317
- 318
- 413
- 414
- 415
- 762
- 640
- 642
- 644
- 3371
- 3799
- 801
- blanc
- 938
- Color Variations 4128

Half cross stitch (2 strands)

- 318
- 415
- 793
- Color Variations 4128

Backstitch (1 strand)

- 318
- 413
- 415 (cubs' eyes)
- blanc

Lion

The splendid lion, particularly the male with his distinctive mane, is one of the most widely recognized animals and is found throughout art and literature. Lions exist wild in sub-Saharan Africa and also in Asia, and have long been kept in captivity in zoos and safari parks. Although the males look impressive, it is the lionesses that do most of the hunting for the pride, using complex and precise teamwork to hunt in grassland and savannah.

After she is about four years old a lioness can bear cubs and will have between one and four young in a secluded den away from the rest of the pride. After about six or eight weeks the mother and cubs return to the pride. Mothers are very protective of their young but will often cooperate with other nursing females to share the job of raising their young. The cubs are playful and mimic stalking behaviour as young as three months but do not begin to join the hunt until about a year old.

What cub could be safer than nestling against his powerful father? The regal qualities of the lion are beautifully portrayed here. A charming second design on page 61 shows the daring playfulness of a young cub.

Pride and Joy

This simple but evocative scene captures a male lion at his most majestic, resting with his young cub. Stitching the design on dark blue Aida conveys the almost limitless stretch of the savannah at dusk.

STITCH COUNT
137h x 168w

DESIGN SIZE
25 x 30.5cm (9¾ x 12in)

YOU WILL NEED
- 46 x 51cm (18 x 20in) 14-count Aida in dark blue (DMC code 336)
- DMC stranded cotton (floss) as listed in chart key (1 skein of each colour)
- Tapestry needle size 24—26
- Suitable picture frame

1 Prepare your fabric and threads for work and mark the centre point on the fabric and on the chart on pages 62–65.

2 Follow the chart and work over one block of Aida, using two strands for whole and three-quarter cross stitches and one strand for half cross stitches. Work backstitches with one strand.

3 When all stitching is complete, check for missed stitches and then remove any guidelines used. Mount and frame your picture as desired.

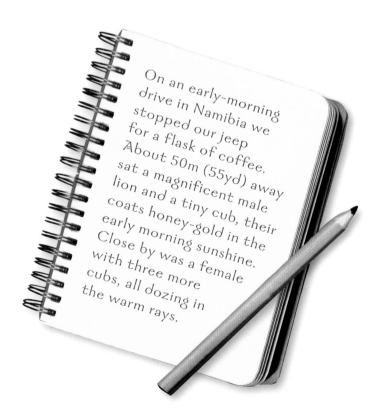

On an early-morning drive in Namibia we stopped our jeep for a flask of coffee. About 50m (55yd) away sat a magnificent male lion and a tiny cub, their coats honey-gold in the early morning sunshine. Close by was a female with three more cubs, all dozing in the warm rays.

Living Dangerously

All young animals love to play and this lively lion cub is no exception – though he'd better hope that mum is in a good mood! The grasses, worked in russet and gold backstitch, help create a realistic environment.

STITCH COUNT
112h x 98w

DESIGN SIZE
20.3 x 17.8cm (8 x 7in)

YOU WILL NEED
🌿 40.5 x 38cm (16 x 15in)
14-count Aida in light blue
(DMC code 800)
🌿 DMC stranded cotton (floss)
as listed in chart key (1 skein
of each colour)
🌿 Tapestry needle size 24–26
🌿 Suitable picture frame

1 Prepare your fabric and threads for work and mark the centre point on the fabric and on the chart on pages 66/67.

2 Follow the chart and work over one block of Aida, using two strands for whole cross stitches and one strand for backstitch.

3 When all stitching is complete, check for missed stitches and then remove any guidelines used. Mount and frame your picture as desired.

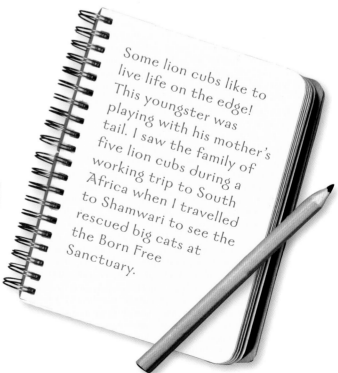

Some lion cubs like to live life on the edge! This youngster was playing with his mother's tail. I saw the family of five lion cubs during a working trip to South Africa when I travelled to Shamwari to see the rescued big cats at the Born Free Sanctuary.

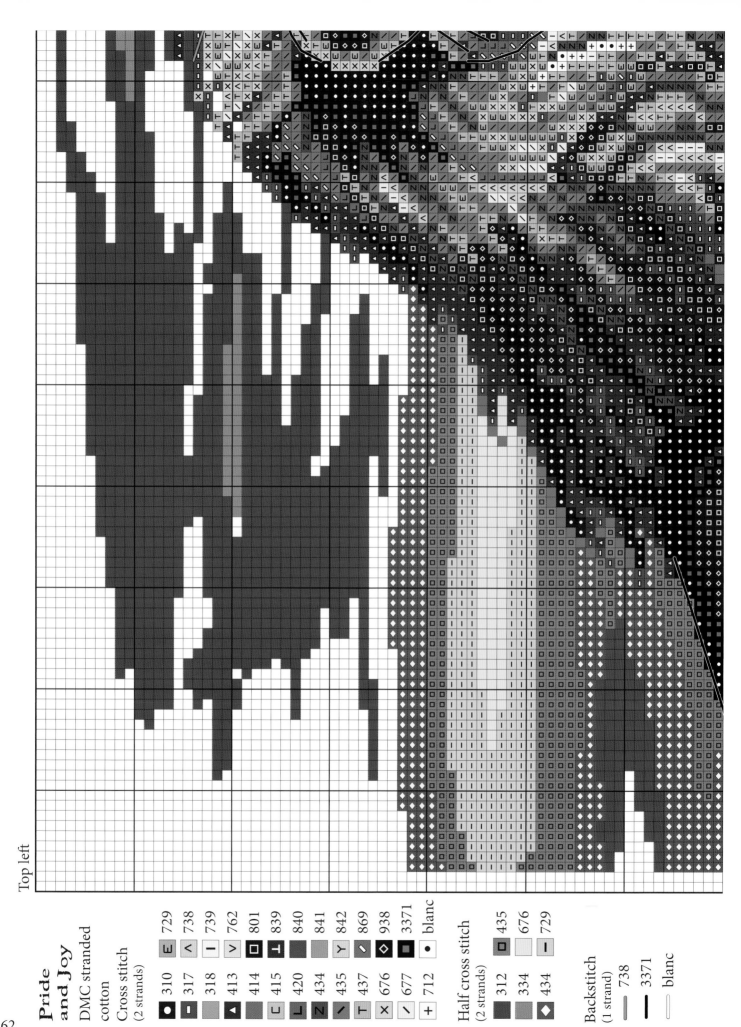

**Pride
and Joy**

DMC stranded
cotton

Cross stitch
(2 strands)

Symbol	Color	Symbol	Color
●	310	E	729
I	317	<	738
	318	—	739
◄	413	∨	762
∟	414	⊡	801
Z	415	⊤	839
⁄	420	■	840
⊤	434		841
✕	435	Y	842
⁄	437	⁄	869
+	676	◈	938
	677	■	3371
	712	•	blanc

Half cross stitch
(2 strands)

Symbol	Color
⊡	312
	334
◈	435
	676
I	729

Backstitch
(1 strand)

Symbol	Color
——	738
▬	3371
—	blanc

62

Bottom left

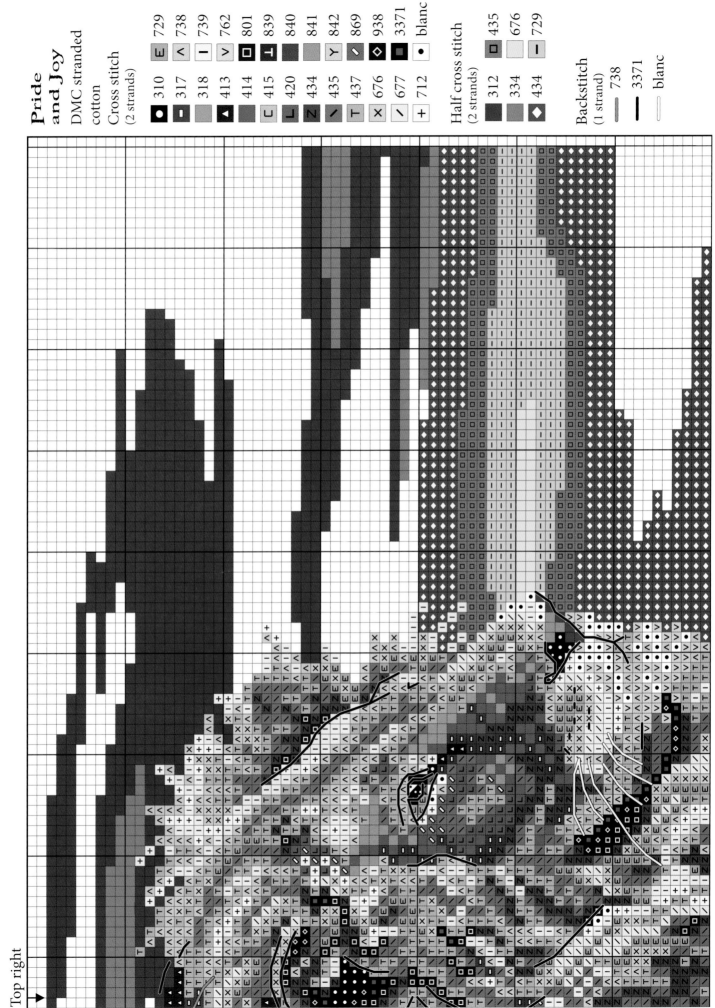

Pride and Joy

DMC stranded cotton

Cross stitch (2 strands)

● 310	E 729
▮ 317	< 738
318	− 739
◀ 413	> 762
414	□ 801
⊥ 415	⊤ 839
L 420	840
N 434	841
╱ 435	Y 842
T 437	╱ 869
× 676	◇ 938
╲ 677	▣ 3371
+ 712	● blanc

Half cross stitch (2 strands)

312	□ 435
334	676
◇ 434	− 729

Backstitch (1 strand)

— 738
— 3371
— blanc

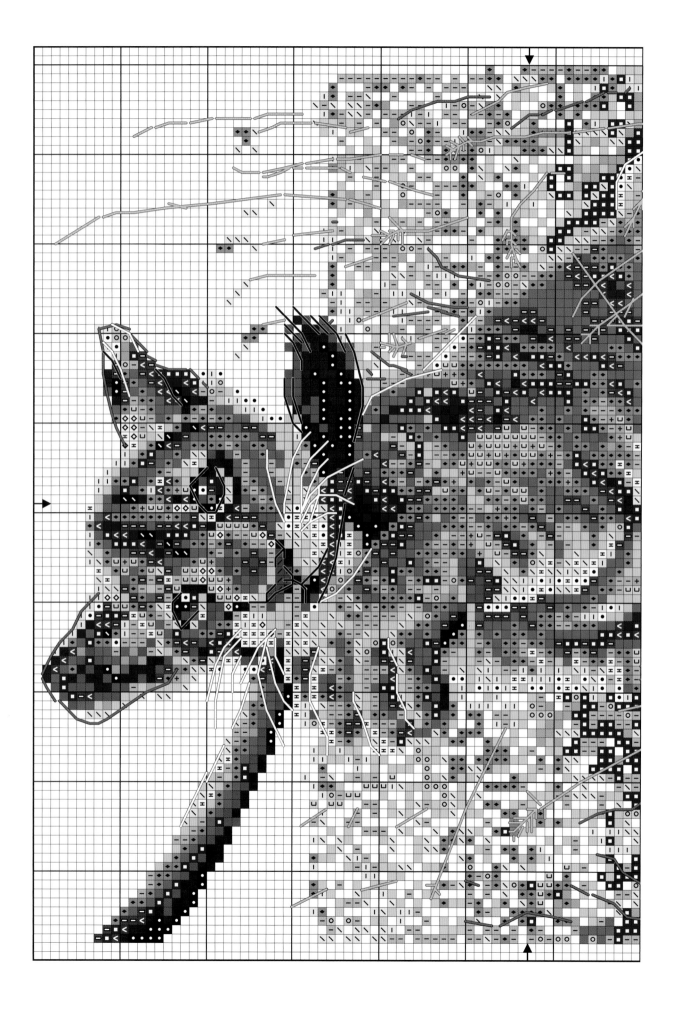

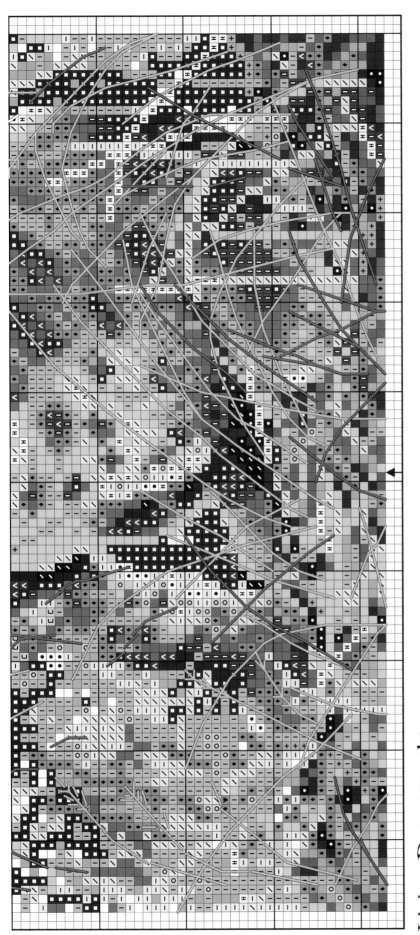

Living Dangerously

DMC stranded cotton

Cross stitch (2 strands)

● 310	H 712	898
317	+ 729	3371
318	738	/ 3862
413	/ 739	● blanc
○ 415	− 762	
433	< 801	
− 434		
435		
◆ 436		
⌐ 437		
⊏ 676		
◇ 677		

Backstitch (1 strand)

413
436
676
blanc

Snow Leopard

The glorious snow leopard is found in the rugged mountainous regions of central Asia. In appearance it is very different from the common leopard and although it has similar black rosettes and broken-spot markings on its coat these are less defined. Its coat is long and woolly, varying from smoky grey to yellowish tan, with white underparts. The tail is long and flexible, helping the leopard to balance on steep, rocky terrain.

The snow leopard is a solitary animal, hunting mainly at dawn and dusk, although male and female may hunt together during the breeding season. The harsh conditions that the snow leopard has to endure means that cubs are born in the spring, to ensure that there is food available. A female usually has between one and four cubs and raises them in the mountains, in a sheltered den that she has lined with her fur. Cubs stay with their mother through their first winter and by the time they are 18 months old they will have learnt from her how to survive in the inhospitable terrain.

The snow leopard's fabulous coat is beautifully displayed in this design. Two little cubs take a cautious peek at the world from behind the protection of their mother.

Peek-a-Boo

What a fun design this is, as two gorgeous snow leopard cubs play peek-a-boo sheltering behind their mother. The distinctive coat patterning of this fabulous feline is shown to best advantage on dark blue fabric.

STITCH COUNT
98h x 126w

DESIGN SIZE
17.8 x 23cm (7 x 9in)

YOU WILL NEED
- 38 x 43cm (15 x 17in) 14-count Aida in dark blue (DMC code 336)
- DMC stranded cotton (floss) as listed in chart key (1 skein of each colour)
- Tapestry needle size 24–26
- Suitable picture frame

1 Prepare your fabric and threads for work and mark the centre point on the fabric and on the chart overleaf.

2 Follow the chart and work over one block of Aida, using two strands for whole cross stitches and two strands for half cross stitches. Work backstitches with one strand. If desired, you could change the stitching direction in the eyes and use Satin thread, as described on page 88.

3 When all stitching is complete, check for missed stitches and then remove any guidelines used. Mount and frame your picture as desired.

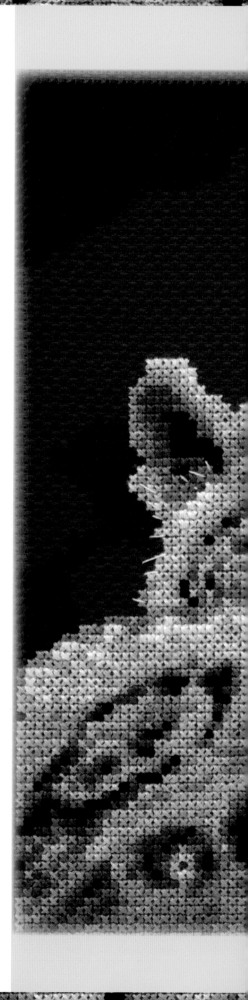

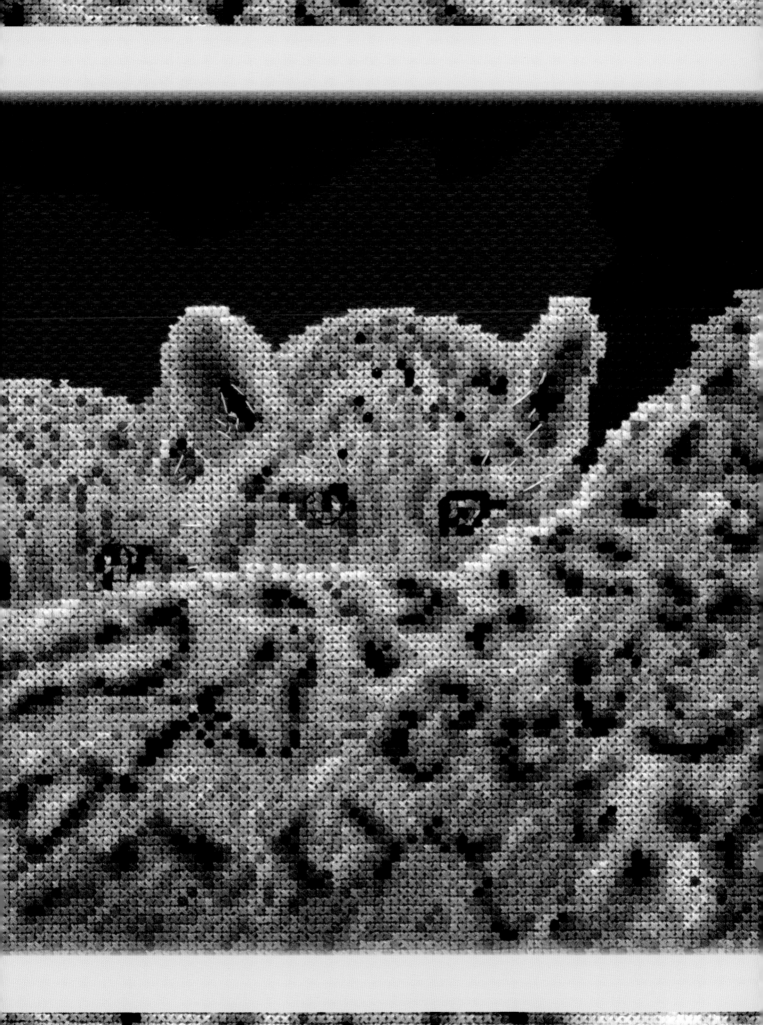

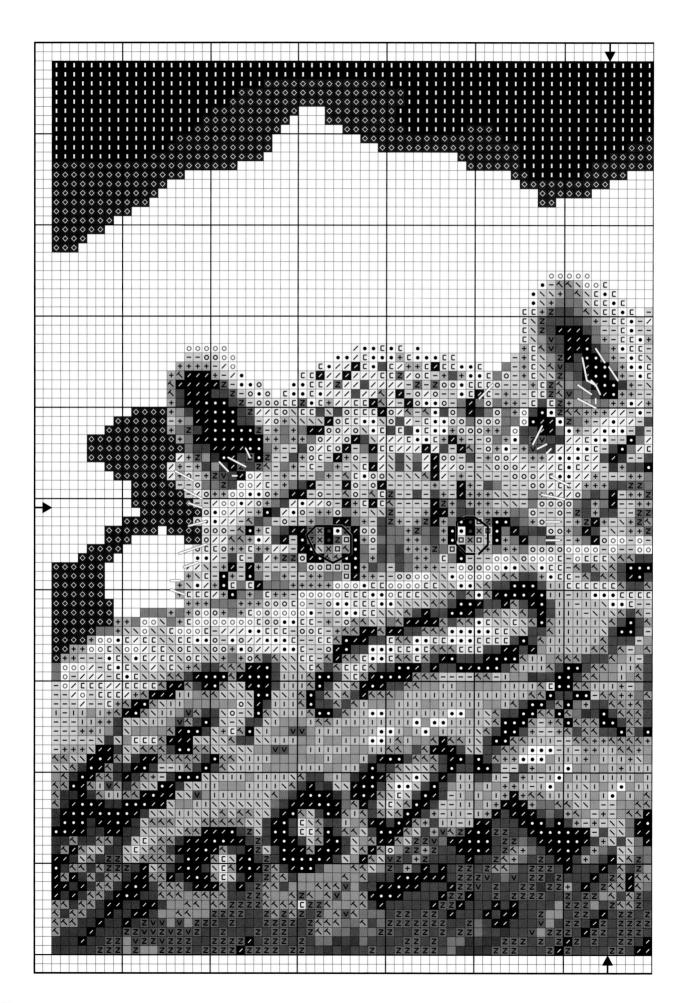

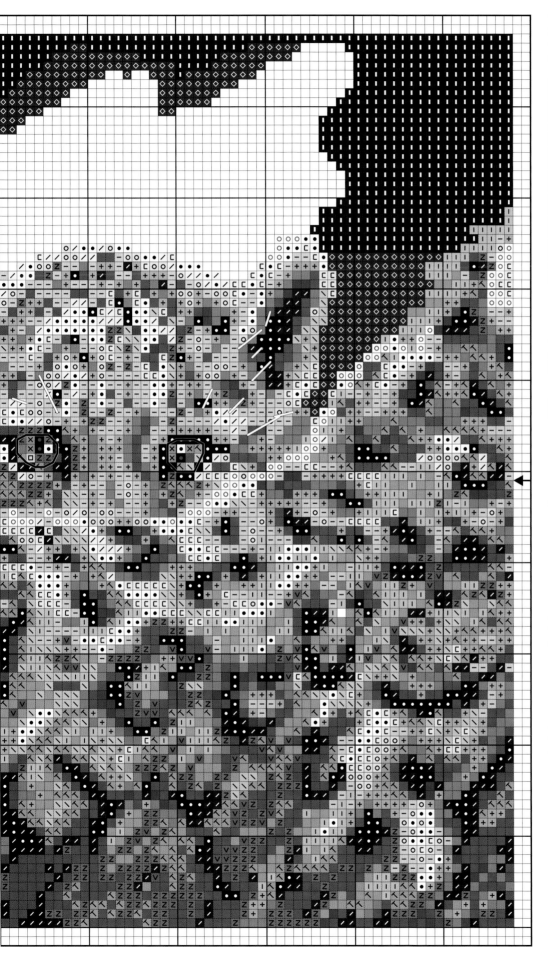

Peek-a-Boo

DMC stranded cotton
Cross stitch (2 strands)

⤚	169
●	310
●	S310 Satin
■	317
╱	413
z	414
╲	415
v	640
■	642
I	644
⊏	762
□	S800 Satin
■	841
×	S841 Satin
■	931
+	932
■	3750
−	3752
O	3753
╱	3756
•	blanc
○	B5200 (3 strands)

Half cross stitch
(2 strands)

◇	823
▌	939

Backstitch
(1 strand)

▬	310
═	blanc

Elephant

The magnificent elephant is the largest land animal on earth and appears in many cultures throughout the world, being noted for its memory and intelligence. An elephant's trunk is perhaps its most distinctive feature and it plays an important role in many activities, from grasping food and drinking, to interacting socially with other elephants. In the mother-calf relationship it is also used to comfort, protect and convey affection.

Elephants may live for up to 70 years and have a very structured society, with the males living mostly solitary lives and the females forming a large, close matriarchal group led by the eldest female. The gestation period for a female elephant is 22 months and at birth her calf will weigh around 120kg (260lb). A new calf is greeted excitedly by the whole herd and is touched and caressed by the adults. The mother selects several full-time babysitters, called allomothers, to help her take care of the calf during its long childhood – it may take 14 years for a male elephant to leave the female herd.

The strong and highly affectionate bond between an elephant mother and her calf is renowned the world over, and this adorable portrait shows why these extraordinary creatures are so admired.

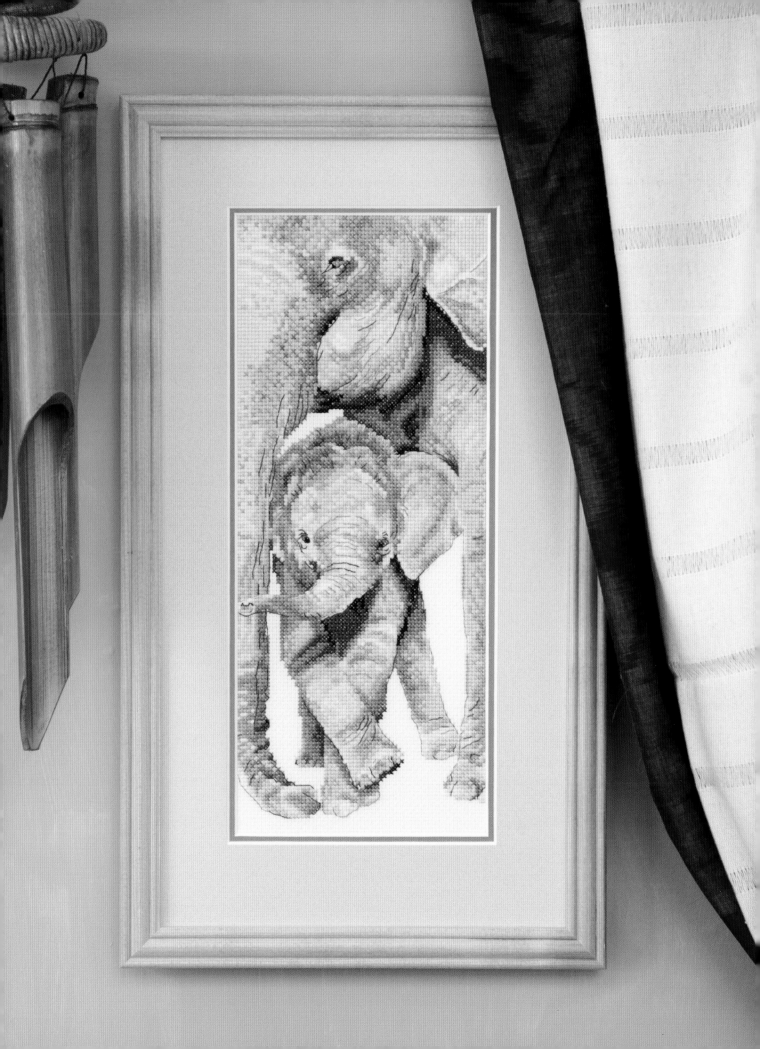

Mummy and Me

This design is simply irresistible. His legs may still be a bit wobbly but this little calf couldn't be safer as he shelters beneath his attentive mother, knowing the herd is in close proximity nearby.

STITCH COUNT
163h x 70w

DESIGN SIZE
29.5 x 12.7cm (11¾ x 5in)

YOU WILL NEED
- 51 x 33cm (20 x 13in) 14-count Aida in ecru (DMC code 712)
- DMC stranded cotton (floss) as listed in chart key (1 skein of each colour and 2 skeins of 415 and 318)
- Tapestry needle size 24–26
- Suitable picture frame

1 Prepare your fabric and threads for work and mark the centre point on the fabric and on the chart overleaf.

2 Follow the chart and work over one block of Aida, using two strands for whole and three-quarter cross stitches. Use one strand for backstitches.

3 When all stitching is complete, check for missed stitches and then remove any guidelines used. Mount and frame your picture as desired.

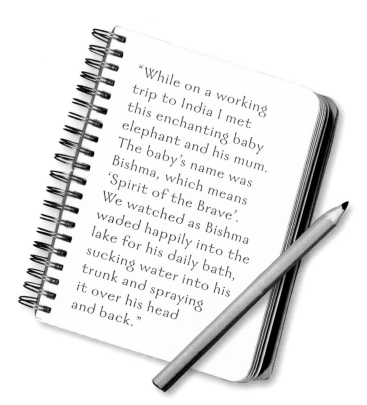

"While on a working trip to India I met this enchanting baby elephant and his mum. The baby's name was Bishma, which means 'Spirit of the Brave'. We watched as Bishma waded happily into the lake for his daily bath, sucking water into his trunk and spraying it over his head and back."

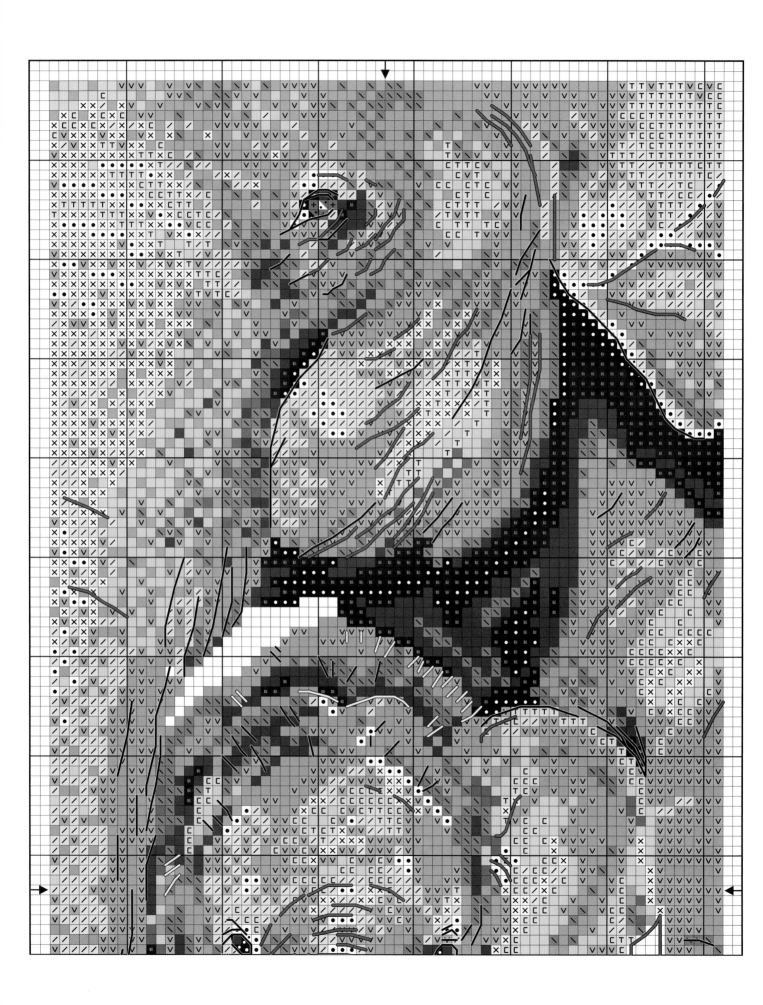

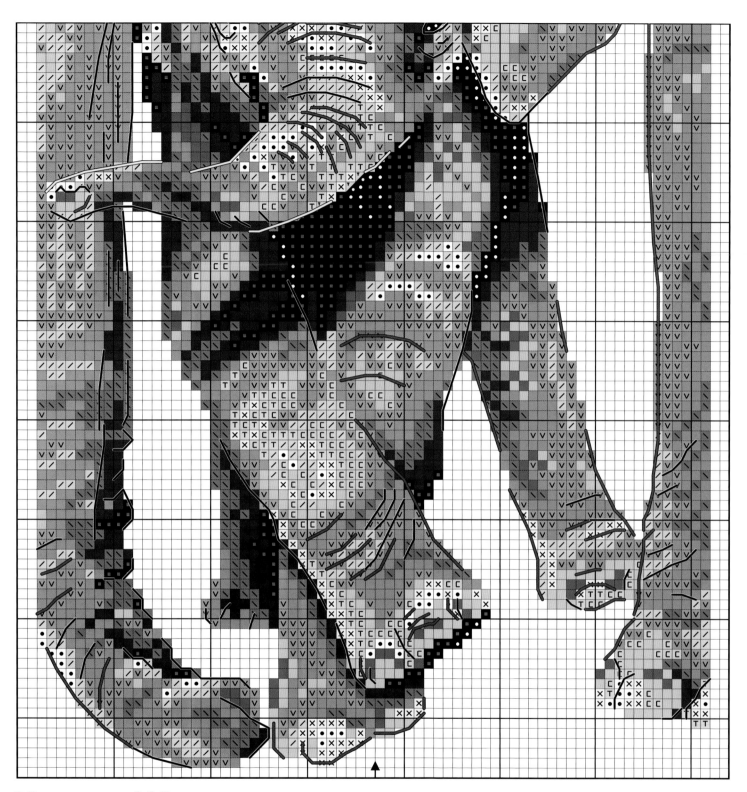

Mummy and Me

DMC stranded cotton

Cross stitch (2 strands)

● 310	◪ 414	⊏ 543
■ 317	V 415	∕ 762
318	+ 435	841

842	✕ 3866
T 3033	● blanc
▣ 3799	

Backstitch (1 strand)

— 414

— 3799

◠ blanc

Giraffe

The giraffe must be one of the most instantly recognizable animals, with its distinctive long neck, highly patterned coat and graceful movements. These sociable and non-territorial creatures live in loose herds in the savannah regions of Africa where they browse on trees.

Female giraffes usually bear their first young when they are around four years old and the minimum interval between calves is about 16 months. During the first week after birth the mother guards her calf very carefully and mothers with calves tend to group together and watch out for each other, resulting in crèches of up to nine calves. The bond between mother and baby is a tight one and although the young are nutritionally independent by about 16 months old, this close relationship with their mother lasts until they are nearly two years old. During that time the mothers are very defensive and have been known to stand over their offspring and defend them from lion attack, delivering well-aimed kicks at the predator.

Giraffes are fascinating creatures that never fail to capture the imagination or the camera lens. The mother-baby bond is a close one and is beautifully portrayed in this charming design.

Loved from Top to Toe

This adorable design captures the essence of the African savannah perfectly with a palette of tawny golds and browns. The marbled Aida fabric coupled with areas of half cross stitch create the lovely blue sky.

STITCH COUNT
168h x 70w

DESIGN SIZE
30.5 x 12.7cm (12 x 5in)

YOU WILL NEED
- 51 x 33cm (20 x 13in)
  14-count Aida in blue marble
  (DMC code 3325)
- DMC stranded cotton
  (floss) as listed in chart key
  (1 skein of each colour and
  2 skeins of 3325)
- Tapestry needle size 24–26
- Suitable picture frame

1 Prepare your fabric and threads for work and mark the centre point on the fabric and on the chart overleaf.

2 Follow the chart and work over one block of Aida, using two strands for full and three-quarter cross stitches. Use two strands for half cross stitches and then work backstitches with one strand.

3 When all stitching is complete, check for missed stitches and then remove any guidelines used. Mount and frame your picture as desired.

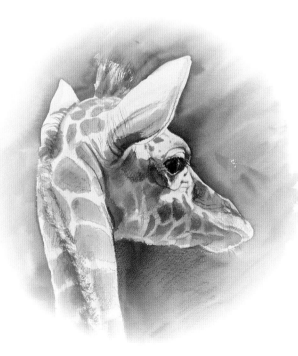

"I will never forget seeing a giraffe on my first safari into East Africa: I could not imagine how an animal standing 5m (16ft) tall could be camouflaged, yet they blended so well with the shapes of the trees that it took me a while to realize they were in front of me! I love painting their huge, liquid eyes and incredibly long eyelashes."

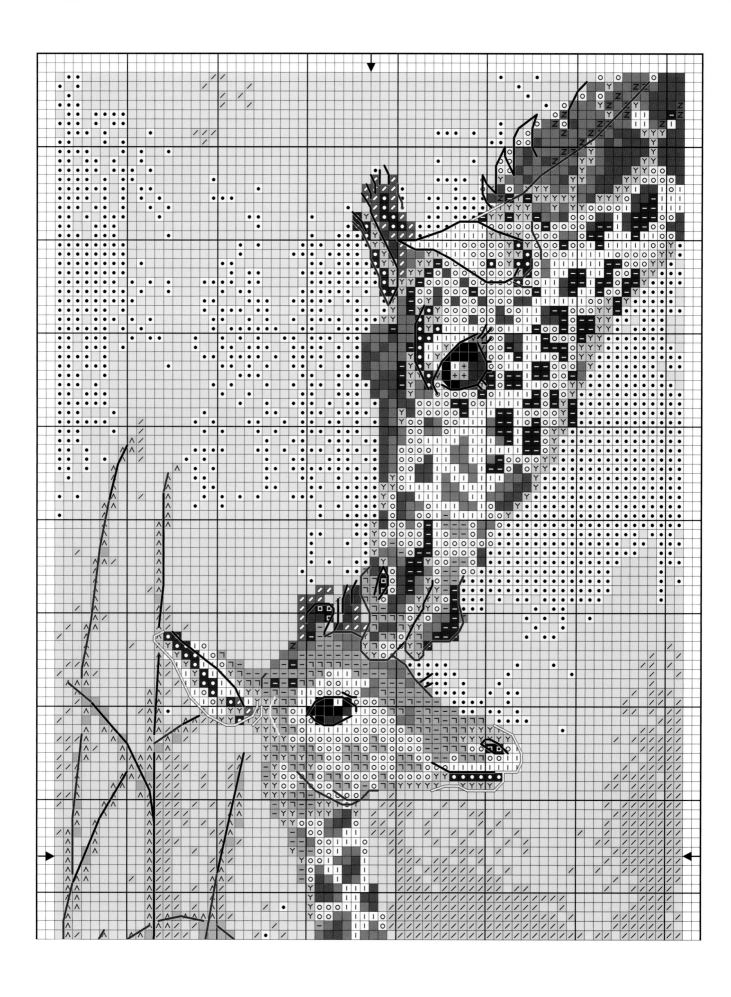

Loved From Top to Toe

DMC stranded cotton

Cross stitch (2 strands)

■ 420	✔ 640	⊖ 832	I blanc			
⊓ 422	v 642	833				
Z 435	Y 644	∧ 834				
T 436	645	▣ 844				
× 437	680	▬ 869				
⊙ 610	○ 712	+ 794				
611	− 729	■ 3371				

Half cross stitch (2 strands)

160	
╱ 519	
• 775	
H 3013	
╲ 3047	
3325	

Backstitch (1 strand)

──── 434
� 677
──── 3371

Cheetah

With its long legs and slender body, the superb cheetah is built for speed, using this advantage to chase and bring down prey. This amazing animal can reach speeds of over 97km/hr (60mph) and can accelerate to this speed in mere seconds. A cheetah relies on tall grasses for camouflage, so favours open savannah and can be found in east and south-west Africa and Iran.

Female cheetahs are solitary animals, whereas males, often brothers, may live and hunt in small groups. A female usually gives birth to between three and five cubs and raises them alone, guarding them vigilantly and moving them often to protect them from danger. When born, cubs do not have the distinctive spotted coat of their mother but are a smoky colour with a woolly mantle along their backs, which may help conceal them from predators. At about six weeks the cubs begin eating from their mother's kills and for the next year or so they learn vital survival and hunting skills from her before beginning life on their own at about 18 months old.

The beautiful cheetah is a skilled huntress and a devoted mother. This stunning family portrait shows their fabulous coat pattern and the distinctive 'tear' stripes on their faces.

Brave New World

This warm and atmospheric design is a wonderful interpretation of the close bond between a mother cheetah and her cubs.

STITCH COUNT
140h x 168w

DESIGN SIZE
25.5 x 30.5cm (10 x 12in)

YOU WILL NEED
- 46 x 51cm (18 x 20in) 14-count Aida in marble yellow (DMC code 677)
- DMC stranded cotton (floss), Satin thread and Color Variations thread as listed in chart key (1 skein of each colour and 2 skeins of 436 and 437)
- Suitable picture frame

1 Prepare your fabric and threads for work and mark the centre point on the fabric and on the chart overleaf.

2 Follow the chart and work over one block of Aida, using two strands for whole and three-quarter cross stitches. To make the eyes appear more three-dimensional the satin cross stitches in the eyes have been worked in different directions to catch the light. For the mother cheetah, stitch the white cross stitch in one eye as normal, but reverse the direction in the other eye so the top diagonal is in the other direction. Do the same with the cubs' eyes. Work backstitches with one strand.

3 When all stitching is complete, check for missed stitches and then remove any guidelines used. Mount and frame your picture as desired.

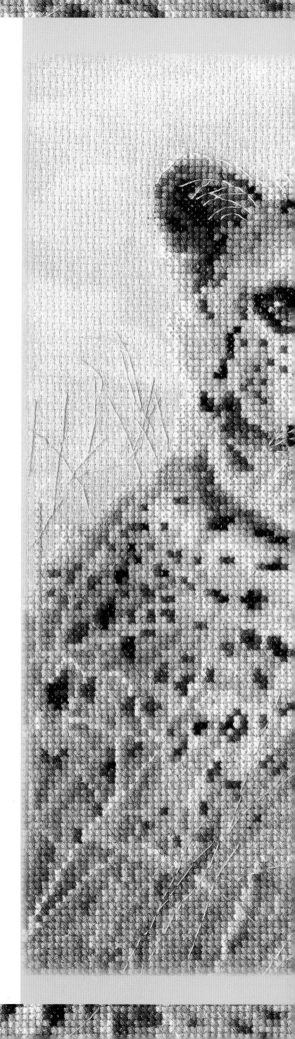

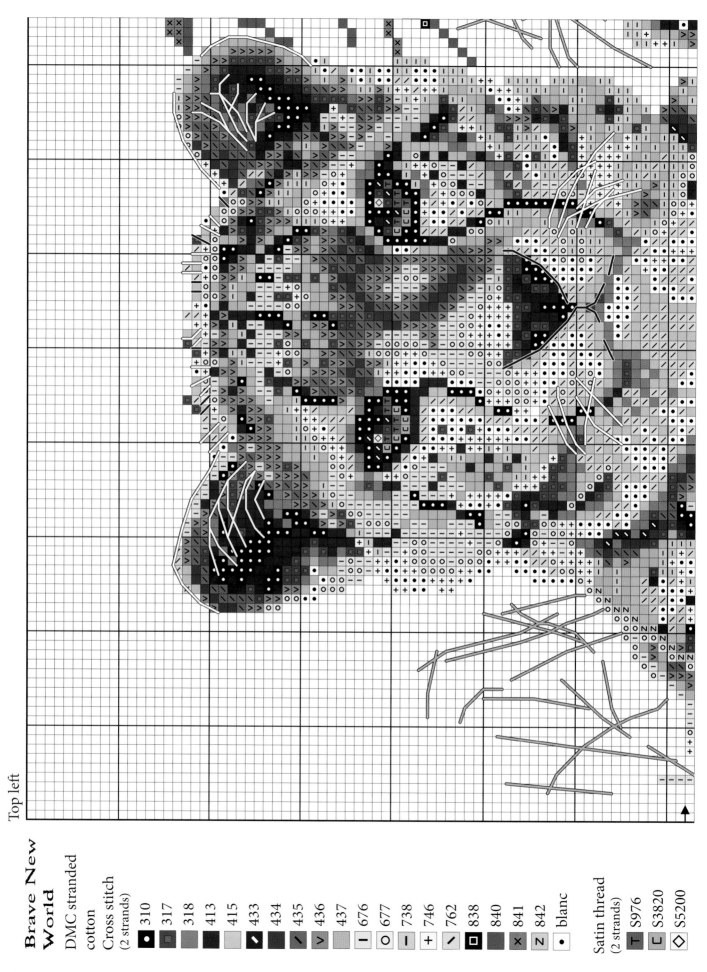

Brave New World

DMC stranded cotton

Cross stitch
(2 strands)

●	310
▣	317
▨	318
◆	413
◢	415
◩	433
◣	434
>	435
—	436
○	437
I	676
+	677
∕	738
▣	746
▨	762
×	838
N	840
●	841
	842
	blanc

Satin thread
(2 strands)

T	S976
⊏	S3820
◇	S5200

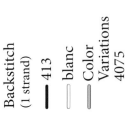

Backstitch
(1 strand)

— 413

— blanc

— Color
Variations
4075

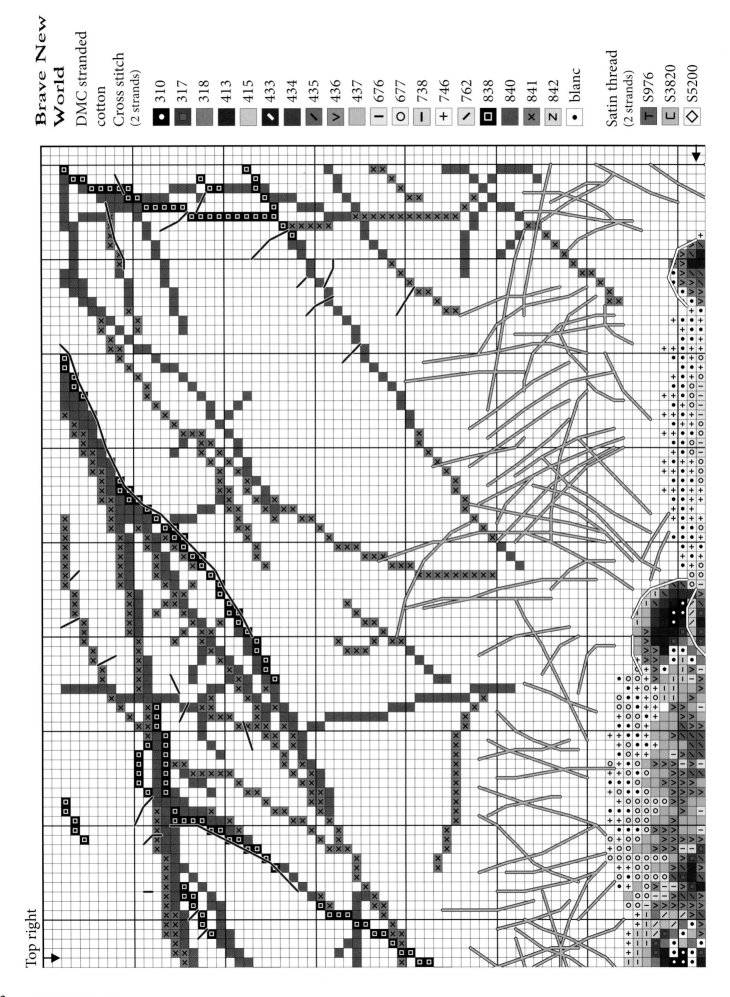

Brave New World

DMC stranded cotton

Cross stitch
(2 strands)

●	310
■	317
	318
	413
	415
◆	433
	434
\	435
V	436
	437
—	676
O	677
I	738
+	746
/	762
□	838
	840
×	841
Z	842
●	blanc

Satin thread
(2 strands)

T	S976
⊔	S3820
◇	S5200

Top right

Backstitch
(1 strand)

413
blanc
Color
Variations
4075

Bottom right

Meerkat

Meerkats are a fascinating type of mongoose found in South Africa. They are very sociable, intelligent animals and live in underground burrows in groups called a mob, gang or clan, which can have as many as 50 members. Each clan has a dominant alpha male and female and mating in the group is usually between them.

When ready to breed, the alpha female will chase away other females that can bear young, to make sure her position can't be threatened and that her young receive the full attention of the clan. These beta females are allowed back into the group once the pups are born and will help feed and protect them. The usual litter size is five or six pups and when they are three weeks old they venture outside the sleeping chamber, where other females in the group will act as babysitters to watch over them. Indeed, meerkats will often risk their own lives to protect the young and if retreat from danger is not possible a female will cover the young with her body.

This wonderful design captures meerkat behaviour perfectly – standing tall, watching out for danger and zealously guarding the inquisitive young pups.

On the Look Out

This delightful design captures perfectly a group of meerkats, with the two adults alert and ready to warn the pups of danger. The design is stitched on a soft green marbled Aida, which creates a realistically hazy atmosphere.

STITCH COUNT
136h x 112w

DESIGN SIZE
24.7 x 20.3cm (9¾ x 8in)

YOU WILL NEED
- 46 x 40.5cm (18 x 16in) 14-count Aida in soft green marble (DMC code 3024)
- DMC stranded cotton (floss) as listed in chart key (1 skein of each colour)
- Tapestry needle size 24–26
- Suitable picture frame

1 Prepare your fabric and threads for work and mark the centre point on the fabric and on the chart overleaf.

2 Follow the chart and work over one block of Aida, using two strands for whole cross stitches, half cross stitches and French knots. Work backstitches with one strand.

3 When all stitching is complete, check for missed stitches and then remove any guidelines used. Mount and frame your picture as desired.

"Some years ago I sat transfixed watching a group of meerkats on sentry duty atop a termite mound in Namibia. Each member of the group appeared to have a clearly defined job, and teamwork was obviously the key to their survival – with hunters, babysitters, lookouts and guards in attendance. I couldn't wait to paint them!"

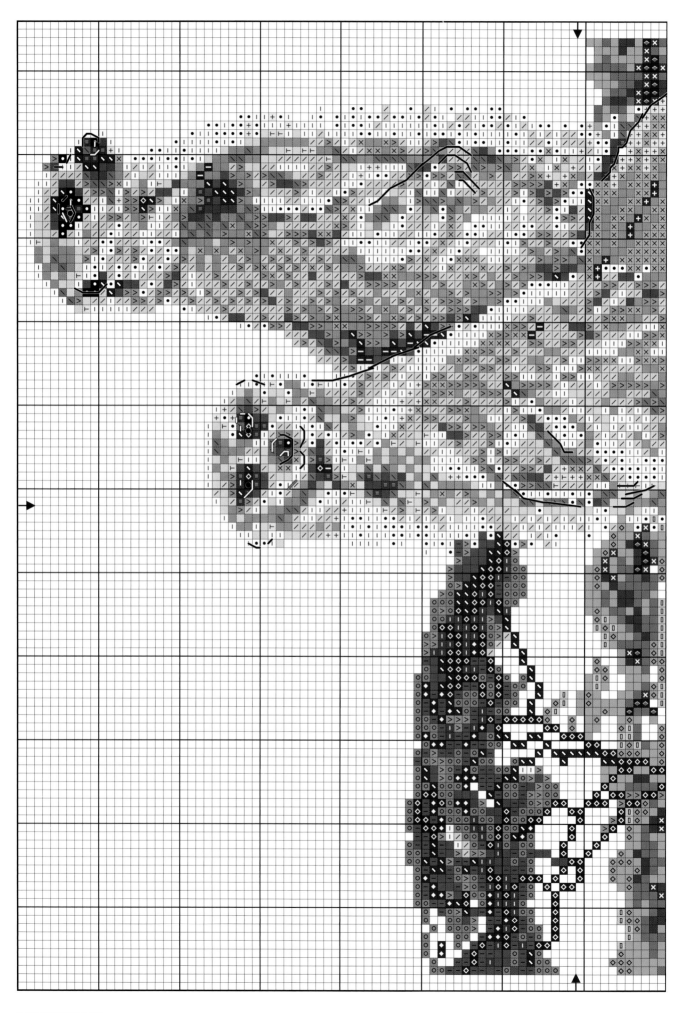

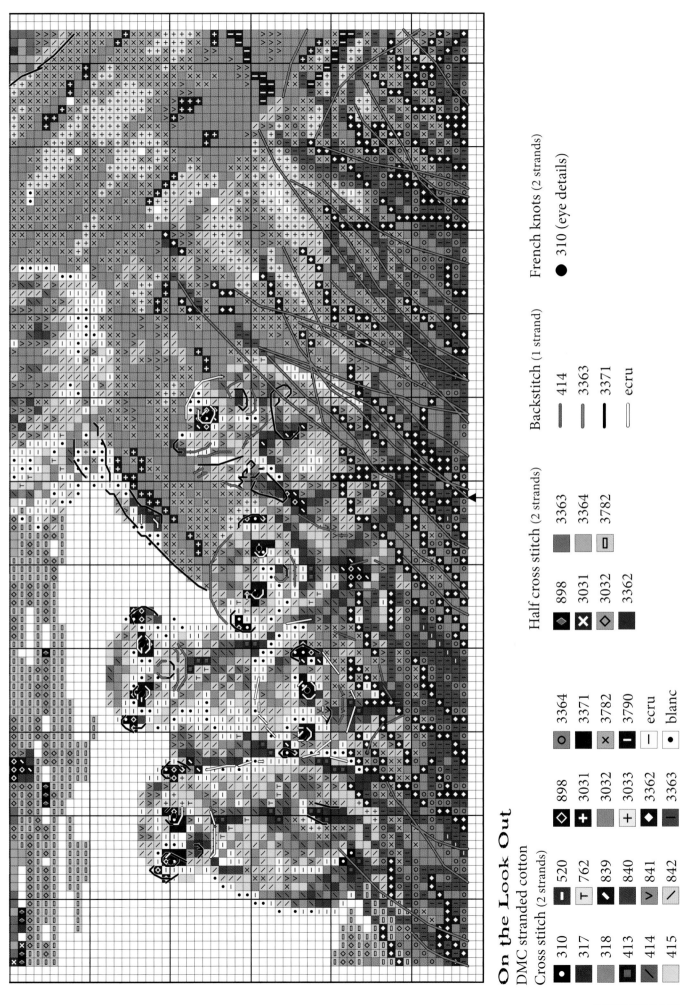

On the Look Out

DMC stranded cotton

Cross stitch (2 strands)

◉ 310	▯ 520	◆ 898	○ 3364
■ 317	⊤ 762	✚ 3031	■ 3371
▨ 318	◣ 839	■ 3032	✕ 3782
▣ 413	▨ 840	✚ 3033	▬ 3790
╱ 414	▷ 841	◆ 3362	— ecru
▨ 415	╱ 842	▮ 3363	• blanc

Half cross stitch (2 strands)

◈ 898	▨ 3363	
✕ 3031	▨ 3364	
◇ 3032	▯ 3782	
▬ 3362		

Backstitch (1 strand)

— 414
— 3363
— 3371
— ecru

French knots (2 strands)

● 310 (eye details)

Materials, Techniques & Stitches

This section is useful to beginners as it describes the materials and equipment required and the basic techniques and stitches needed to work the projects. Framing pictures is described overleaf. Refer to page 104 for DMC contact details.

Materials

Fabrics

Most of the designs in this book have been worked on 14-count Aida fabric, with three designs worked on 16-count Aida and one design on 28-count linen. You could work the 16-count Aida design over two threads of 32-count linen if you prefer. You could also work any of the designs over a smaller or larger gauge (count) of fabric but be aware that if you change the gauge of the material, that is the number of holes per inch, then the size of the finished work will alter accordingly – see Calculating Stitch Count and Design Size below.

Threads

The projects have been stitched with DMC threads, including stranded embroidery cotton (floss), Satin threads, Color Variations threads and Light Effects threads. These threads are available as six-stranded skeins, which can easily be split into separate strands. The project instructions and chart keys tell you how many strands to use. Some projects require more than one skein of a colour, so check before you buy.

Needles

Tapestry needles, available in different sizes, are used for cross stitch as they have a rounded point and do not snag fabric. Sizes 24–26 are normally used.

Scissors

You will need two pairs of scissors: a pair of dressmaking shears for cutting fabrics and a small pair of sharp, pointed embroidery scissors for cutting and trimming threads.

Frames

It is a matter of personal preference as to whether you use an embroidery frame or hoop to keep your fabric taut while stitching. Generally, working with a frame helps to keep the tension even and prevent distortion, while working without a frame is faster and less cumbersome. There are various types on the market – look in a DMC catalogue and also in your local needlework store.

Techniques

Preparing the Fabric

Spending a little time preparing your embroidery fabric before stitching will save you time and trouble in the long run and produce superior results.

- Before starting work, check the design size given with each project and make sure that this is the size you require for your finished embroidery. Your fabric must be larger than the finished design size to allow for making up, so allow 10cm (4in) to both dimensions when stitching a picture or sampler and 5cm (2in) to both dimensions for smaller projects.

- Before beginning to stitch, iron the fabric if necessary to remove creases and then neaten the fabric edges either by hemming or zigzagging to reduce fraying as you stitch the design.

- Find the centre of the fabric. This is important regardless of which direction you work from, in order to stitch the design centrally on the fabric. To find the centre, fold the fabric in half horizontally and then vertically, then tack (baste) along the folds (or use tailor's chalk). The centre point is where the two lines of tacking meet. This point on the fabric should correspond to the centre point on the chart. Remove these lines when work is completed.

Calculating Stitch Count and Design Size

Each project gives the stitch count and finished design size but if you want to work the design on a different count fabric you will need to re-calculate the finished size. Being able to work out the eventual size of a design means that you can decide how much fabric you need for a particular project or whether a design will fit a specific picture frame or card.

Stitch Count To work out the stitch count, first count how many stitches there are along the height of a design and then along the width (don't forget to count any backstitches or French knots too on the outer edge of a design).

Finished Design Size To work out the finished design size, divide each of the stitch count numbers by the fabric count of the embroidery fabric you want to use. For example, a design 140 stitches high x 70 stitches wide worked on 14-count Aida is $140 \div 14 = 10$ inches and $70 \div 14 = 5$ inches. So the finished stitched design will be 10 x 5in (25.5 x 12.7cm). When calculating design sizes for evenweave fabrics, divide the fabric count by 2 before you start, because evenweave is worked over two threads not one block as Aida.

Using Charts and Keys

The charts in this book are easy to work from. Each square on the chart represents one stitch. Each coloured square, or coloured square with a symbol, represents a thread colour, with the code number given in the chart key. Most of the designs also use half cross stitches. A few of the designs use fractional stitches (three-quarter stitches) to give more definition to the design. Solid coloured lines show where backstitches or long stitches are to be worked. French knots are shown by coloured circles.

Each complete chart has arrows at the sides to show the centre point, which you could mark with a pen. Where the charts have been split over several pages, the key is repeated. For your own use, you could colour photocopy and enlarge charts, taping the parts together.

Starting and Finishing Stitching

It is always a good idea to start and finish work correctly, to create the neatest effect and avoid ugly bumps and threads trailing across the back of work.

To finish off thread, pass the needle through several nearby stitches on the back of the work, then cut the thread off, close to the fabric.

Knotless Loop Start Starting this way can be very useful with stranded cotton (floss), but only works if you are intending to stitch with an even number of threads, i.e., 2, 4, or 6. Cut the stranded cotton roughly twice the length you would normally need and separate one strand. Double this strand and thread your needle with the two ends. Pierce your fabric from the wrong side where you intend to place your first stitch, leaving the looped end at the back of the work. Return your needle to the wrong side after forming a half cross stitch and pass the needle through the waiting loop. You can now begin to stitch.

Away Waste Knot Start Start this way if working with an odd number of strands or when using variegated threads. Thread your needle and make a knot at the end. Take the needle and thread through from the front of the fabric to the back and come up again about 2.5cm (1in) away from the knot. Now either start cross stitching and work towards the knot, cutting it off when the threads are anchored, or thread the end into your needle and finish off under some completed stitches.

Washing and Pressing

If you need to wash your finished embroidery, first make sure the stranded cottons are colourfast by washing them in tepid water and mild soap. Rinse well and lay out flat to dry completely before stitching. Wash completed embroideries in the same way. Iron on a medium setting, covering the ironing board with a thick layer of towelling. Place stitching right side down and press gently.

The Stitches

Backstitch

Backstitches are used to give definition to parts of a design and to outline areas. Some designs use different coloured backstitches. To work backstitch follow Fig 1, bringing the needle up at 1 and down at 2. Then bring the needle up again at 3, down at 4, and so on.

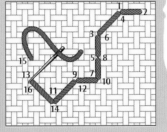

Fig 1 Working backstitch

Cross Stitch

A cross stitch can be worked singly over one block of Aida (Fig 2a) or over two threads of linen or evenweave fabric. A half cross stitch is simply a single diagonal line.

To make a cross stitch over one block of Aida, bring the needle up through the fabric at the bottom left side of the stitch (number 1 on Fig 2a) and cross diagonally to the top right corner (2). Push the needle through the hole and bring up through the bottom right corner (3), crossing the fabric diagonally to the top left corner to finish the stitch (4). To work the next stitch, come up through the bottom left corner of the first stitch and repeat the sequence.

You can also work cross stitch in two journeys by working a number of half cross stitches in a line and completing the stitches on the return journey (Fig 2b). For neat work, always finish the cross stitch with the top stitches lying in the same diagonal direction.

Fig 2a Working a single cross stitch on Aida

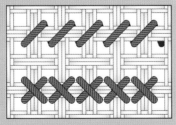

Fig 2b Working cross stitch in two journeys

Three-quarter Cross Stitch

Three-quarter cross stitches give more detail to a design and can create the illusion of curves. They are shown by a triangle within a square on the charts. Working three-quarter cross stitches is easier on evenweave fabric than Aida (see diagram). To work on Aida, make a half cross stitch from corner to corner and then work a quarter stitch from the other corner into the centre of the Aida square, piercing the fabric.

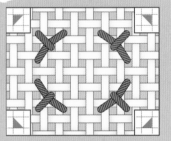

Fig 3 Working three-quarter cross stitch

French Knot

French knots have been used as highlights and details in some of the designs, in various colours. To work, follow the diagram, bringing the needle and thread up through the fabric at the exact place where the knot is to be positioned. Wrap the thread twice around the needle, holding the thread firmly close to the needle, then twist the needle back through the fabric as close as possible to where it first emerged. Holding the knot down carefully, pull the thread through to the back leaving the knot on the surface, securing it with one small stitch on the back.

Fig 4 Working a French knot

Making Up

The cross stitch designs in this book have all been made up as framed pictures but you could make them up in other ways, such as wall hangings and cushions, or use smaller parts of the designs for greetings cards.

Mounting and Framing Embroidery

It really is best to take large samplers and pictures to a professional framer, where you can choose from a wide variety of mounts and frames that will best enhance your work. The framer will be able to stretch the fabric correctly and cut mounts accurately in various shapes. If you intend to mount the work yourself, use acid-free mounting board in a colour that will not show through the embroidery and follow the method described below.

1 Cut a piece of mount board to fit the frame aperture (draw around the frame's backing board). Using double-sided tape, stick a piece of wadding (batting) to the mount board and trim the wadding to the same size using a sharp craft knife.

2 Lay the embroidery right side up on to the wadding, making sure the design is central and straight, matching a fabric thread along the edges. Push pins through at the four corners and along the edges to mark the position. Trim the fabric to leave 5–10cm (2–4in) all around.

3 Turn the embroidery and mount board over together. Stick double-sided tape around the edges of the board to a depth of 5cm (2in) and peel off the backing. Fold the excess fabric back, pressing down firmly to stick the fabric to the board, adding more tape to neaten the corners. Remove the pins and reassemble the frame with the embroidery in it. It is not necessary to use the glass; this often flattens the stitches when they are pushed against it.

Tips for Perfect Stitching

Cross stitch is one of the easiest forms of counted embroidery. Following these useful pointers will help you to produce neat and attractive work.

🍂 Before starting, check the design size given with each project and make sure that this is the size you require for your finished embroidery. If the design is to be mounted in a picture frame the fabric you are stitching on should be at least 20cm (8in) larger all round than the finished size of the stitching, to allow for making up.

🍂 Organize your threads before you start a project as this will help to avoid confusion later. Put the threads required for a project on a thread organizer and always include the manufacturer's name and the shade number.

🍂 When you have cut the length of stranded cotton (floss) you need, usually about 46cm (18in), separate out all the strands before taking the number you need, realigning them and threading your needle.

🍂 If using a hoop, avoid placing it over worked stitches and remove it from the fabric at the end of a stitching session.

🍂 For neat cross stitching, work the top stitches so they all face in the same direction.

🍂 If your thread begins to twist, turn the work upside down and let the needle spin freely for a few moments.

🍂 If adding a backstitch outline, add it after the cross stitch has been completed to prevent the solid line of the backstitch being broken.

DMC Fabrics, Threads, Kits & Contacts

DMC Fabrics

DMC have various types of fabric available for cross stitch and other forms of embroidery and some of the most popular are described here.

DMC Aida

Aida fabrics are usually made from cotton and are woven with the threads grouped in bundles to form a square pattern. Aida fabric is easy to work with, especially for beginners. It is available in pre-cut shapes and by the metre in a wide range of colours and in various gauges or counts – 6, 11, 14, 16 and 18. The count or gauge of a fabric determines how many stitches can be worked per inch (2.5cm), so the higher the count, the more stitches to the inch.

DMC Evenweave

Evenweave fabrics are made of cotton and various fibres and are woven with single threads. These fabrics are available in a wide range of colours, in pre-cut pieces or by the metre. Cross stitch is normally worked over two threads of evenweave and the counts available are 25 and 28.

DMC Linen

This fabric is made from 100% linen, is woven from single threads and, like evenweave, is normally worked over two fabric threads. It is available in various colours in 28- and 32-count.

DMC Aida and Evenweave Bands

Bands are very useful as trims, to personalize accessories and for quick-stitch projects. They are available in various widths, colours and counts and with different decorative edgings.

DMC Threads

Many different types of lovely threads are available from DMC. The designs in this book use stranded cotton (floss), Color Variations thread, Satin thread and Light Effects.

DMC Stranded Cotton

This six-stranded divisible thread is perfect for stitching on all types of fabric and is available in a choice of 465 colourfast colours. It is double mercerized to give it an attractive gloss comparable to silk.

DMC Color Variations

These six-stranded divisible threads are available in 36 multicoloured or tone-on-tone shades. Used like stranded cotton, every six or seven stitches reveal a different colour.

DMC Satin

These six-stranded threads are silky soft and bring a shimmering brightness to cross stitch and other embroidery designs. There are 36 washable and lightfast colours available. Colour codes for these threads begin with S.

DMC Light Effects

These six-stranded divisible speciality threads are available in 36 glistening colours to add light and reflective qualities to needlework projects. There are six different thread 'families' – gold and silver, precious stones, antique gilt finishes, precious metal effects, pearlescent effects and fluorescent effects. Colour codes for these threads begin with E.

DMC Kits

A DMC kit has everything you need to create beautiful cross stitch projects, including needle, fabric, threads, chart and any accessories the design requires. All kits have clear and easy-to-follow instructions. New kit designs are always being added, so refer to an up-to-date DMC catalogue to see all of the wonderful Pollyanna Pickering designs that are currently available. Your local needlecraft store should have a catalogue or go to www.dmccreative.co.uk. In the catalogue you will find a wealth of other cross stitch designs in kit form, suitable for all skill levels.

DMC kit code BK191

DMC kit code BK725

DMC Accessories

There are many accessories available to make cross stitch and other forms of embroidery easier and more pleasurable and DMC have a wide range of useful items, a few of which are shown here. A DMC catalogue will show you the full range available – ask at your local needlework store or go to the DMC website at www.dmccreative.co.uk.

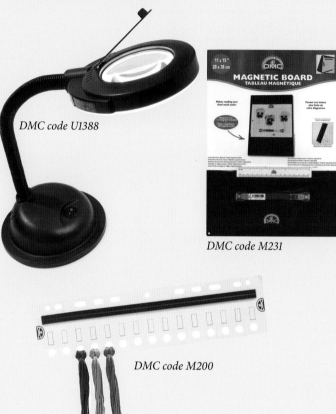

DMC code U1388

DMC code M231

DMC code M200

DMC Contacts

UK
DMC Creative World Ltd
1st Floor Compass Building, Feldspar Close, Enderby, Leicestershire LE19 4SD
Tel: 0116 275 4000
www.dmccreative.co.uk

USA
The DMC Corporation
South Hackensack Avenue, Port Kearny Building, 10F South Kearny, NJ 07032
Tel: 1 973 589 0606
www.dmc-usa.com

FRANCE
DMC
5 Avenue de Suisse, BP 89, 68314 Illzach Cedex
Tel: (33) 0389 319189
www.dmccreative.co.uk

Pollyanna Pickering Books

Giant Pandas and Sleeping Dragons, Anna-Louise Pickering, Otter House (Licensing) Limited, 1996

On Top of the World, Anna-Louise Pickering, Otter House (Licensing) Limited, 2001

A Brush with Wildlife, Anna-Louise Pickering, Otter House (Licensing) Limited, 2004

The Eye of the Tiger, Anna-Louise Pickering, Otter House (Licensing) Limited, 2007

To purchase books and related Pollyanna Pickering products contact: sales@otterhouse.co.uk
Otterhouse Limited, Water Lane, Haven Banks, Exeter EX2 8BY, UK
Tel: +44 (0)1392 427333
www.otterhouse.co.uk

 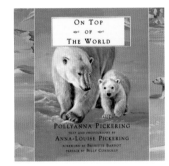  

Index